AFFIRMATIONS

By the same author
COMMENTARY ON THE SUNDAY AND
PRINCIPAL HOLY DAY READINGS

AFFIRMATIONS

BASED ON THE

SUNDAY

AND PRINCIPAL HOLY DAY

READINGS

ASB YEAR ONE AND TWO

John Fenton

The Canterbury Press
Norwich

First published 1993 by The Canterbury Press Norwich
(a publishing imprint of Hymns Ancient & Modern Limited,
a registered charity)
St Mary's Works, St Mary's Plain,
Norwich, Norfolk, NR3 3BH

British Library Cataloguing in Publication Data

A catalogue record for this book is available
from the British Library

ISBN 1–85311–071–X

*Typeset by Datix International Limited, Bungay, Suffolk
Printed and bound in Great Britain by
St Edmundsbury Press Limited
Bury St Edmunds, Suffolk*

To the staff and readers
of the *Church Times*

PREFACE

Most of these pieces were published in the *Church Times* between 1991 and 1993; the first was for the 20th Sunday after Pentecost, Year 1, and it appeared in the issue of 4 October 1991. I am very grateful to the Editor, John Whale, for allowing me to gather them together in a book. I have added material for the Sundays that did not occur in the period covered by the series and for the principal Holy Days.

The intention behind these *Affirmations* was to suggest a possible way of proceeding, from the notes on the eucharistic passages in *The Alternative Service Book 1980*, already published under the title, *Commentary on the Sunday and Principal Holy Day Readings* (The Canterbury Press, Norwich, 1991), to a theme that might form the basis for a sermon, address, or homily. It proved more difficult than I had expected, as anyone who compares the two books will see.

I am most grateful to those who have typed sections of the book: Sally Ford, of the Chapter Office, Christ Church; Glenys Macgregor and Jan Bolongaro of the Tutors' Office; and Yolande Clarke of the *Church Times*.

August 1993   John Fenton
                                                                   Wolvercote, Oxford

CONTENTS

ix

CONTENTS

CONTENTS

CONTENTS

ASB YEAR ONE

THE SAVIOUR IS THE MAKER

9th before Christmas
ASB p.398

EVERYBODY (one assumes) is more or less painfully aware of the contrast between what they are, and what they would like to be and believe they should be. Nothing seems to make the contrast less painful – certainly not time, which only convinces us all the more of the distance between the reality and what is expected of us.

One way to seek relief is by putting the blame for the situation on someone else. We did not ask to be the sort of people we are; it is not our fault that we are like this. If God wanted us to be loving and generous and forgiving, why did he not make us so in the first place? It is rather as though there were two offices in our local authority, and we were playing one of them off against the other; when we received bills from one of them, we sent back our excuses and complaints about the other: how can we possibly meet this demand, when we have never had the wherewithal to pay?

The doctrine that Christ, our saviour, is also the one through whom God made everything, comes to our help at just this point. There are not two separate departments, making and saving; we cannot excuse ourselves to one, by complaining about the other. God has always dealt with us through the one Christ, both in making us and in saving us. There is no possibility of bureaucratic muddle in God. His dealings with the world are elegant and economical.

Also, of course, and for this reason, they are full of hope for us. There is no room for despair; not even for anxiety or disquiet about ourselves, our faults, and our peculiar and habitual tendencies. What will be redeemed is what was made by the redeemer himself, and not by someone else. He will not say of us, There is

3

nothing to be done with this kind of workmanship, except throw it away and start again with an entirely new model. He is our alpha and our omega; what he redeems is what he created, and what he created he will redeem; he remains responsible for us, from beginning to end.

The belief that Christ is both maker and saviour has this effect upon us: it means that we can relax. The painful awareness of our shortcomings – of not being what we should be – is dealt with; it is removed. Indeed we did not ask to be made like this, but the one who made us like this is God, the same God who had a perfect creature in mind right from the beginning, and who will get us there, in the end.

The faults and weaknesses in our characters are to be seen as areas of hope and gaps to be filled with glory – sites for future development, where the most stunning filling-in will take place. When we were children, they used to say to us, Fools and daft people should not see things half-done. We are only half-made, so far; it will come right in the end.

ALL IN THE MIND

8th before Christmas
ASB p.403

THE teaching of Jesus in today's gospel (Mark 7.14–23) as to what it is that separates us from God, is very clear and, if we can grasp it, very encouraging. Alienation from God, he says, comes from what we think; it makes its bridgehead in our minds. Our unacceptable behaviour is the result of the way we think; if we could stop thinking the way we do, we should stop acting the way we do, and we should then be obeying the will of God, and living in union with him.

Experience shows us that this is indeed exactly how it is. We are commanded to love our neighbour, but we find that we do not; and when we examine ourselves to find out why we do not, we see that the cause lies in what we think: fear, envy, jealousy, lust and so on. If we could change our thoughts, we could change our actions. What we want is to be transformed by the renewal of our minds (Romans 12.2).

Our destructive thoughts about our neighbours flourish on ignorance. If we knew them better, we should not think about them in this way. The danger lies in lumping them together in a faceless category: foreigners, the rich, the poor, Catholics, Protestants, Fundamentalists. The renewal of our minds will involve and require getting to know some of the people about whom we are so negative, and discovering that they are not as bad as we had thought; individuals are far more lovable than classes.

The reason why the teaching of Jesus, that what defiles us is what goes on in our minds, is so encouraging, is because we have the assurance that the Holy Spirit works in our thoughts. He changes the way we think. If our unholiness is the result of unholy ideas, then our holiness will be the result of holy ideas, and these will be the work of the Holy Spirit.

It would no doubt be an exaggeration, but a good exaggeration, to say, It is all in the mind. Our uncharitable actions come from thinking one way; our charitable actions will come from thinking another way. And this other way is a possibility: I can risk getting to know the people I fear, despise and hate, because there is the Holy Spirit who will change my ideas. He is the God of the interstices, and he will reveal my neighbour to me as one whom I can love.

THE JOKE IS ON US

7th before Christmas
ASB p.407

D ARE ONE say it? – The comedians are far nearer to the truth than the theologians. The church is, and always has been, the subject of ridicule; and rightly. From Paul's admission that he was being very foolish (2 Cor. 12.11) to Anthony Trollope's portrayal of clergymen in Barsetshire, and so on. The infinite distance between what the church believes itself to be, and what it manifestly is and does, is enough to inspire an unending series of jokes.

But the humour of the situation goes further than the differences between the visible and the invisible. Even if there were no churches to laugh at, nor any clergymen or other religious persons often apparently unaware of their ridiculousness, the thing that is to be believed makes fools of us; as Paul knew, it is the folly of the gospel that saves those who have faith (1 Cor. 1.21).

But the joke is older than Paul. It goes right back to Genesis, and the stories about the birth of Isaac, whose name means, He laughs (Genesis 17.19 REB footnote). Sarah says, God has given me good reason to laugh, and everyone who hears will laugh with me (21.6); because one does not usually associate the birth of a child with parents, one of whom was a centenarian and the other a nonagenarian. God had made them look ridiculous; he had spoken about Abraham's family, but there had been no child by Sarah; he had put them in the position of wanting a child and trying to have one, but kept them waiting until all reasonable expectation should have come to an end long before. Now, it happens, and they laugh, he laughs, and everybody else laughs with them.

Paul, with superb insight, lights on this as the archetypal example

6

of faith (Romans 4. 13–25). The old man, still hoping and carrying on because God had promised that there would be a son, is the model for all who believe in the resurrection of the dead Jesus. To be a believer is to be a fool, like Abraham; and to laugh at yourself for doing it, and to be laughed at by everybody else.

What impresses us most about holiness is not the discipline that is involved, nor the serious-mindedness of it, nor the wisdom of the saints, nor their charity, but their humour. You see it in their eyes. If it is not there, you know that there is something essential that is missing. But how can anyone be so amused, in a world like this? It is clearly not hard-heartedness; they are the most caring and loving people. In some extraordinary way they can see more than we can see: not just the world of hunger and thirst and homelessness and tragedy, which is clearly visible to everybody; but something else as well – the humour of it all. Comedians know it too, far better than theologians.

HUNGER FOR LIFE

6th before Christmas
ASB p.413

THE PROBLEM with the readings for this Sunday is not that Christian writers of the first century compared Jesus to Moses: God sent Moses to lead the Hebrews out of slavery in Egypt into Canaan, and he sent Jesus to bring us from death to life. Our problem is that we find it difficult to give much meaning to the idea that what we need now is redemption, and a redeemer to do it for us. It was obvious to the Hebrews in Egypt (and to anyone reading the story in Exodus 3.7–15) that if they were to get out, they would need a leader who would organize them. It was also, apparently, obvious to people in the first century that what they needed was salvation (hence the question, What must I do to be saved?); and there were plenty of people willing to prescribe answers. In what direction should we look, to see any evidence that what we need is somebody to help us out of a desperate situation – what the collect calls, The tyranny of sin and death?

Both the story of Moses and the story of Jesus include incidents in which the leader provides food for his hungry followers; and it may be that we can get some light on our problem through concentrating on this idea: hunger and food.

We have to eat, in order to live. All living things are subject to this rule. We are not the sort of machines (if there are any) that process their own fuel indefinitely. We have to ingest, frequently. Most of us, at least once a day; many of us, more frequently than that. It may sound over-dramatic to say that we live all the time on the edge of starvation; but it is only the presence of our abundance of food that conceals this from us. If anyone does not believe it, try it out: no solids, no liquids, for the next 24 hours, and see if it is not so.

This is only the beginning of the understanding that we are in search of; hunger for food is a sign that points to something else: our needs that are for a different sort of satisfaction. The weakness of a starving person points to the weakness of our wills; we know what we should do, in many cases, but we are not able to do it. We do not organize our lives in relation to the needs of other people; we do not do the things that must be done if the world is to become a better place for people to live in.

Before we can ask the question, How can this man save us? we have to ask another, Is there anything we need to be saved from? Our permanent need of food and drink is a perpetual reminder of our need of a redeemer – a nudge towards the idea of our own and our society's hunger for the bread that gives life to the world.

Nor do we need to go far from the idea of the need for food: the world we live in is a hungry world, and part of the problem is our lack of will to feed it. If we cannot see that, whatever shall we see?

THE SEVERITY OF GOD

5th before Christmas
ASB p.417

PAUL TELLS US to observe the kindness and the severity of God (Romans 11. 13–24): the kindness we think about often, and it is pleasant to do so; he forgives our sins, he accepts us as his family, and he promises us eternal glory. But the severity of God is a different matter altogether; we hope that he will not be severe with us, and leave it at that, maybe.

But maybe we should not leave it at that. Certainly Paul did not think we should. He instructed his readers in Rome to observe both the kindness and the severity of God: severity to those who fell away. He was thinking of the Jews who had not believed in the gospel, the natural branches in his parable of the olive, that had been lopped off. The same thing could happen to Gentile believers, if they fell away from faith. Put away your pride, he says to them, and be on your guard – or, to translate it more literally: Do not think high things, but be afraid.

He will say it again in the next chapter: Do not be proud, but be ready to mix with humble people (12.16). This shows us what he has in mind; God's severity is aimed at those whose high opinion of themselves makes them incapable of associating with those who seem to them inferior.

It would be one thing to think high things about ourselves, if these were the things that God has done for us, in making us, and saving us, and promising us his glory. Ideas like this would not make it difficult for us to associate with other people. What Paul is against is the high things we think about ourselves that assure us that we are better than most other people: more intelligent, more perceptive, holier and more God-like.

There is nothing intrinsically wrong with having a good self-image; everything depends on what it is made of. If it is the kind that lives on ideas such as, At least I don't do what they do; I'm certainly better than those people – it will keep us from mixing with those whom we despise. And this is the test: Does your idea of yourself isolate you from other people, or does it encourage you to associate with them?

The severity of God is fixed against pride. He wants to shatter our false self-esteem. Arrogance is what he cannot take. It is not difficult to see why. There can be no place for it in the holy city.

SURE HOPE

Advent Sunday
ASB p.422

WE SAY, I dare to hope; as though hoping were a risky business that required exceptional courage. This is not how it is with the Advent Hope which is the theme of this Sunday's readings. Hope is inevitable for those who have faith in a God who is good; you cannot believe in God without expecting him to do something, everything, to put things right. Hope is a consequence of faith, and it is as sure as faith.

Stuck in a train that has stopped in a tunnel, one might say, I do not know exactly what will happen, but my faith in British Rail will not allow me to think that we shall be here for ever. Surely something will happen. And when we say Surely, we mean that we are sure that it will happen.

Faith in God, the author and sustainer of everything that exists, the one who is wholly good and fair, as well as infinite in skill and ingenuity, forces us to think: There must be a future, in which everything will come right. The fact that we cannot describe how it will come about or what it will be like does not prevent or restrict our hoping or our longing; on the contrary, it makes us long and hope all the more. But our inability to describe it does not mean that there is absolutely nothing that we can say about it.

What will be must be better than what is. It would be impossible to believe in a good God who was going to make things worse for his creatures. It is hard enough to accept that he has allowed there to be so much suffering now; it would be contrary to everything we believe about him to think that he will make the future even worse.

Moreover it is difficult to think that he can ever fail, in the smallest degree or the slightest respect. To fail is human not divine. God's wisdom, skill ard ingenuity must be such that he can have no write-offs, dead ends, or total disasters.

Faith in God as the Creator who cares about his creation requires us to have a comparable hope. There must be a completely satisfactory future, with no place for regrets or disappointments. All tears will be wiped away. We cannot see how it will happen, but that does not matter, how it will happen is not our business. What we can see, without any doubt or hesitation, is that it must happen. God must be God to everything.

THIRSTY FOR RIGHTEOUSNESS

2nd in Advent
ASB p.426

R EADING the Old Testament is like eating salted peanuts: it makes you thirsty. The thirst that the Old Testament produces is for justice; to see right prevail (Matthew 5.6). Again and again, as we read the Hebrew histories, we think that God's kingdom is about to come and his will about to be done on the earth; but hope is always postponed: every judge is followed by a period of national disobedience; Solomon is led astray by his wives and the kingdom is divided after his death; the promises of return from exile are never fulfilled on the scale we had been led to expect; the Maccabean victories soon turn sour. The biblical writers know what should be, but they also know that it has not yet happened as it should.

What is true on the national and world-wide level is also true on the level of the individual. There are no perfect people. Abraham, Jacob, Joseph, Moses, Aaron, David – all have flaws in their characters and failures in their lives; and the Hebrew authors do nothing to conceal it from us.

No wonder, therefore, that the prophet addresses his hearers as those who are thirsty (Isaiah 55.1), and no wonder that the beatitudes declare the blessedness of those who hunger and thirst and mourn.

They shall be satisfied. The future tense is important. We are not be be satisfied with what is here, now; but perpetually dissatisfied with it. Advent is important because it rubs our noses in the future. No amount of reconciliation now, of present justification, of the presence of Christ with us till the end of the age; no abiding in Christ or living in God and God living in us, is enough for what we want. They are only peanuts, compared with what is still to come, and what we are to long for; that is, that God's name will be honoured by every creature that he has made; that his rule will begin and bring prosperity, life and joy to all; that his will and purpose will be achieved at last. Finish your creation, we say; renew everything you have made; make it work perfectly.

We can, of course, thank God for our faults; what else can we do with them? But we can only thank him, on the understanding that they are reminders, to us and to him, of unfinished business. They increase our dissatisfaction with what we are, and our longing for the day when they will exist no more. God is like the builders who do half the job and then go off to work on another site. We ring them up every week: When will you come and complete the work you began and clear up the mess?

ATTEND TO WHAT IS SAID

3rd in Advent
ASB p.432

THE fourth evangelist has already told us what to expect from the Baptist: He came as a witness to testify to the light, so that through him all might become believers (John 1.7). We wait to see how he will do it, but what he says immediately contradicts our expectations.

The deputation of priests and Levites from Jerusalem asks the obvious question, Who is this person who is speaking about someone who will come after him? What authority has he to speak in this way? By what title should we understand him? John replies with three thunderous negatives: I am not the Messiah. I am not Elijah. I am not the Prophet. Witnesses have no status of their own; they stand only by the truth of that to which they bear witness. All John will say is that he is a voice, and that he prepares for another; we knew that already.

The negative answers of the Baptist (so firmly fixed in our memories by Orlando Gibbons' anthem, This is the record of John) overthrow the expectations of the Jerusalem deputation, and our own expectations; they also surprise us, because they seem to contradict the identification of John with Elijah that Mark (9.13) and Matthew (17.13) both make. To bear witness is enough by itself; we do not need to ask, Who are you?, or What right have you to say this? To raise the question of a person's authority is frequently a way of avoiding paying attention to what the person has to say.

Is this why we know nothing for certain about any of the four evangelists, or about many of the other authors of New Testament books? Even Paul is hardly an exception, since we cannot be certain how many of the letters attributed to him were by him; and in any case he had no obvious authority to speak, as his opponents were quick to point out. We would be none the wiser if we knew more about the origin of the New Testament, and we are none the worse for our ignorance. The function of the writers is to testify: to point away from themselves to what is to be believed. There is wisdom in the words of an old author:

> Do not be influenced by the importance of the writer, or whether his learning be great or small, but let the love of pure truth draw you to read. Do not enquire 'Who said this?' but pay attention to what is said.

(If this is so, then it is unnecessary to record the name of the author of this quotation. But, just in case anyone wants to read more of his wise sayings, the write is Thomas à Kempis, in *The Imitation of Christ*, Book I, chapter 5.)

LET IT HAPPEN TO ME

4th in Advent

ASB p.436

THE two accounts of the Annunciation, one in Matthew's gospel and the other in Luke's, differ from one another with regard to the point of view from which the stories are told: in Matthew, the angel of the Lord speaks to Joseph; in Luke, Gabriel appears to Mary. Matthew says nothing at all about the attitude of Mary to the events that are being foretold by the angel; but in Luke, Mary says: Behold I am the handmaid (literally, slave-girl) of the Lord; let it be to me according to your word. She has been told what will happen; she submits to God's will.

It is difficult to know what should be said about our relationship to God's grace. Do we co-operate with it, or do we submit to it? Different responses may be appropriate at different times, but one thing is sure: there are occasions and situations in which the only possible response is submission; and when that is the case, it is important that we should do so.

At some point in our lives, the course that they will take begins to be predictable; we see what sort of people we shall be, what kind of work we shall do, whether we shall be married or single, whether we shall have children or not, and if we shall, what they will be like. In many of these areas, what will happen is unlikely to change; and the question is, Shall we submit, or shall we resist?

Both are possible courses of action. We know people who have attempted to resist what seems inevitable, and have fought against it and refused to accept it. And sometimes this has proved right in the end, and they have achieved what they wanted to achieve. On the other hand, we know people who have submitted to what they believed to be inevitable, and we wondered whether resistance might not have been the better course.

There is only one thing in this difficult area of which we can be at all certain, and that is that if we are to submit, and submit joyfully and without resentment, it will have to be because we believe that God wills our good, and that he can be trusted.

The whole of Christian faith comes to our aid at this point. There is only one God; he has no rivals. He is the maker of everything; there is nothing he cannot cope with. He raised Jesus from the dead, to assure us of his good will towards us. He gives us the Spirit, so that we can always share his life. He will rule for ever, and be everything to all that exists.

The inevitable is not to be feared, resented or resisted, but accepted, welcomed and affirmed. Gabriel tells Mary what is to happen, and she says, Let it happen to me as you have said.

HE CHANGED THE WAY WE THINK

Christmas day
ASB p.443

CAN one person do anything? If they cannot, why celebrate the birth of one person, as we do on Christmas day?

We do not need to bring on the heavy doctrines to see that one person can do a great deal. It is a common experience that a new member coming into a discussion-group changes the nature of the group; or, more to the point, perhaps, that the birth of a baby alters the life of a family. Certain people have changed the way in which millions have thought: Plato, Karl Marx, Freud, for example. Artists and writers make us see things in a different way: Wordsworth, or van Gogh. On this level, if on no other, we can explain Christmas to ourselves, as the celebration of the birth of a person who changed the way people think.

It is no accident that we celebrate his birth. The way in which he changed our thinking is to do with children, babies, helplessness. There are two moments in which Jesus is helpless: as a baby, and when he is being crucified; Christmas and Good Friday. He changed the way we think about weakness, both the weakness of the young and of the old, by being born of a woman and by being put to death by crucifixion.

Can one person do anything? Here is something that one person has done: as a result of the movement that Jesus began, we think in a different way from people who lived before he was born; we have far more respect for weakness, powerlessness, poverty, decrepitude. We do not think that glory and power are identical: but we reflect on the weakness of God, disclosed both in the birth and in the death of his Son. Moreover we have first-hand evidence that this was a new and unacceptable idea when it was first introduced into human history: Paul, who preached Christ nailed to the cross, said it was an offence to Jews and folly to Gentiles; but that it was, nevertheless, God's power and wisdom (1 Corinthians 1. 18–25).

Jesus has changed our ideas; that is one reason for celebrating his birth.

GOD WITH US

Sunday after Christmas Day
ASB p.450

ISAIAH's prophecy of the name that the women would give her child – Emmanuel, God is with us – was taken up by Matthew and stands as the first example of the fulfilment of prophecy in a book that is rich in this respect. Matthew seems to have wanted to emphasize the belief that Christ never left his disciples, and he balances this first fulfilment with the last words of Jesus, I will be with you always, to the end of time (28.20).

The Christians of the first generation did not think that Jesus had come and gone, like everybody else. Even those who believed, as Matthew did, in the return of Christ as the judge at the end, did not think that he was absent from his followers until he came again; they believed that when they met in his name, he was with them (18.20). The Emmanuel prophecy of Isaiah was, one might say, irresistible to Matthew; it expressed exactly what he believed: God is with us, because Jesus is with us.

Paul also believed in the continuing presence of Jesus in the lives of the believers. God had sent the Spirit of his Son into their hearts, and they knew that this was so, because they said Abba, the Aramaic word that means Father. They addressed God in this way, because of the Spirit which those who believed had received from God.

John, too, believed in the dwelling of the Word among us, and our abiding in him, like branches in a vine. Jesus had come to the disciples on Easter day, and he had given them the Spirit; he had never left them, and he had promised that he never would (John 14.18).

In the collect we ask that we may share the life of Christ's divinity; but to the writers of the New Testament this was not a matter of asking, but the point from which faith starts; a datum, not a petition; something to give thanks for, not something not yet present. We might ask that we should know it more clearly and be more aware of it, but hardly pray for it as though it were not yet the case.

The closeness of God to us and of us to God is like a Christmas present that has been scarcely unwrapped but put away somewhere, in a cupboard, unappreciated. We need to take it out and look at it again. We imagine an immense distance between us and God: he is in heaven and we are on earth. But this was not how the earliest Christians saw it: The Spirit of Jesus was in their hearts – that is, in their minds, their real selves; Jesus was with them and therefore God was with them; they were in God, and God was in them. Distance had been abolished. He was at your elbow and inside your head; Emmanuel.

NOT LIKE US

2nd Sunday after Christmas
ASB p.454

WE NEED not blame ourselves for not understanding God. We should not expect to be able to make complete sense of his ways, or to be forever at peace with him. It is wrong to think that our relationship with him will always be smooth, without crises or times of turmoil. There is a distance between him and us, and it will be so for as long as we are here; we can only see a bit and understand a fraction of what he is about; and we should not be surprised that this is how it is. God is God, and we are very different from him.

In much the same way, those who attend to God most closely

are set apart from the rest of us. We often find their words and actions surprising, inexplicable, maybe even indefensible. They live by a light that we cannot see, and they know things about which we are ignorant. One day we may understand, but at the moment we can only be astonished at their behaviour.

Luke tells us (2.41ff) no more than one story from the time between the infancy of Jesus and his baptism by John, and it is a story of misunderstanding. Both sides are surprised at the behaviour of the other party: Mary says to Jesus, Why have you treated us like this? And Jesus says to her, Did you not know that I was bound to be in my Father's house (or: about my Father's concerns)? This one occasion from the childhood of Jesus that Luke chooses to report teaches the reader of the gospel to expect the central figure of the book (who speaks here for the first time) to be incomprehensible and to say things and do things that leave us bewildered.

What is important to the evangelists is the difference between Jesus and us. They waste no ink on telling us that he was like us; it is hard to think of any passage in any of the four gospels that might have been written with the primary aim of showing that Jesus underwent experiences that were the same as ours, and so that he was truly human. The whole drift of their books, and of the stories and sayings that they contain, is to emphasise how unlike us Jesus was.

The reason why the evangelists saw their task in this way was because they believed in Jesus as the saviour; and to be a saviour of others, you must be different from them; yet another person of the same sort would be no help; it would only add to the problem.

Luke's story of Jesus at the age of 12 makes him stand out from his family and his contemporaries, from the teachers in the temple, from what is expected of 12-year-olds and what seems proper in relation to one's parents. It isolates Jesus and points to what is special about him: he is the one we need.

NO MORE MAGIC

Epiphany
ASB p.460

THE wise men (RSV), or astrologers (REB), or magicians (as the word might be translated), never appear again in Matthew's book. They have served their purpose, in the birth story, and withdraw. Matthew brought them on for two reasons: because they were gentiles, not Jews (coming from the East and asking for the King of the Jews); and because they practised magic. It is a major theme of this gospel that Jews reject Jesus, but gentiles accept him; and it is also made clear that to accept Jesus means to abandon magic and the purpose that magic was supposed to serve.

Magic is a method of getting something done when the doer needs extra strength; it depends on the belief that there are forces that can be called in to achieve one's aims, whether they be good or bad. Spells and curses extend one's will and the power that one has over people and situations. But all such self-will must go, if one is to be a follower of Christ and child of his Father.

He tells his disciples to love their enemies and pray for their persecutors (Matthew 5.44f), not that they may cease to be enemies and persecutors; rather, the disciples are to follow the example of their heavenly Father, who prospers the life of good and bad alike, with sunshine and rain.

We are to love those who hate us, and do good to those who persecute us, in order that they may hate us and persecute us all the more; self-will and self-centredness must go. The magicians have left their money and the tools of their trade in Bethlehem; they could only appear again in the gospel as ex-magicians who had abandoned their evil business. (Compare the same theme in Acts 19.18ff.)

Matthew's story of the magicians means good-bye to all the tricks we use to get our own way: flattery, deceit, enlisting the support of other people's bad motives, lying, force. We should be deeply suspicious of the magic of a personality, our own or anyone else's. Our model is to be God, who loves indiscriminately, making no difference between the innocent and the wicked.

BE BAPTIZED

1st after Epiphany
ASB p.463

GETTING INTO the Jordan to be baptized by John (Matthew 3.13ff) must have been a rich experience for a first-century Jew; you could explain it in many ways. John had said that it was the necessary preparation for the coming age, the time when God would rule the world. His will, only, would be done then. How were you to be ready for such a time? The river Jordan was the chosen place (all the gospels agree on that) and this was no accident; it reminded you of Joshua and the first entrance of Israel into the promised land. They had crossed the river on dry ground. There was no miracle now; you had to get into the water; you had to confess your sins and be washed. You were like Naaman the Syrian, the man with the illness that made you unclean; he had washed in the Jordan, eventually, and been restored; you believed you would be clean, too. God had promised through the prophets that he would cleanse his people before the day of the Lord came; here was John, fulfilling the prophecies. He was Elijah, returned from heaven, still wearing his leather girdle round his waist; Malachi had said he would come before the great and terrible day, and now here he was.

You had to get into the water, John said. (That was why they called him the Baptist.) The element that stood for destruction had to go over you and overwhelm you. The ceremony was an act of submission: to John, to water, to death and destruction, and to God. You could speak of being baptized with a baptism, and mean suffering. You could say, I have a baptism to be baptized with, and mean, I must die. You were handing yourself over to God totally, as one does in death. And you believed that what he gave you back, on the far side of the action, would be forgiveness, cleansing, a new life, the life that was needed to survive the judgement of God and live under his rule in the restored Israel of the new age.

You could not say too much about John. He was certainly the greatest person who had ever lived, because he had brought the news of the coming age and of what to do about it. What you had to do was not strain yourself to do better and be more holy by keeping the law of Moses. What you had to do was to confess your sins, submit to your destruction and accept your resurrection. Die, and be raised up by God. Then you would be able to survive in the new world in which God's will would be done.

The simplicity of it was both terrifying and attractive. Everybody went to John, the gospels say. All the inhabitants of Judaea and of Jerusalem; and Jesus, too.

FOLLOW ME

2nd after Epiphany
ASB p.467

THE FUTURE is largely hidden from us, and it is a mercy that it is so. We would not be able to cope if we knew in advance all that will happen to us; it is bad enough, looking back at the past; but having it all laid out before us in prospect would be unbearable.

The disciples, as they are described in Mark's gospel, are told a little at a time what they are to be and to do. All that is said on the first occasion when they appear is that they are to come with Jesus and that he will make them into fishers of men (Mark 1.16ff). The odd expression tells them very little about what is to be involved; only that instead of fishing for fish, they will fish for people. What were they to make of that? They caught fish to kill them and sell them for food; they made money out of fish.

It is hard to think that the metaphor was to be pressed further than the one point of comparison: they had dealt with fish in the past; in the future they were to deal with human beings instead.

Mark's gospel shows how what they are to be and do is disclosed to them (and to the reader of the book) gradually; the only way in which they (or we) could possibly receive it. In chapter 3 we are told that the Twelve are to be with him and that they will be sent out to preach and to have power over demons. The sending out is in chapter 6; they preach repentance, cast out demons and heal the sick.

They must, however, be broken before they can be effective, and Mark shows us how they are reduced to misunderstanding Jesus, making mistakes and false moves, being rebuked and in the end abandoning him altogether after being warned that this is what will happen. The final picture of Peter, their leader, is this: And he burst into tears (14.72). They cannot really be with him, if they are still with themselves; self is one of the things that will have to be lost, if they are to do what they have been appointed to do.

The disciples are to do what Jesus does. He proclaims the coming rule of God, and they are to do so, too. He casts out demons and so do they. He heals the sick, and they heal the sick. But to do what Jesus does is not to imitate his actions; it involves more than that. They must be transformed, changed internally, become different people. Just as the Son of Man must suffer, so must they, in order that they may become what he is: bearers of the Spirit; no longer themselves, but new beings, with new names.

The words that Mark uses – Come with me, follow me, be with me – conceal the awful truth: what happens to Jesus in Mark's gospel, must also happen to his disciples. Mercifully, we only realize this when it is too late.

SHAME AND GLORY

3rd after Epiphany
ASB p.471

JESUS revealed his glory by performing signs, and the first of these signs was at Cana in Galilee, where the wine ran out at a wedding, and Jesus turned water into better wine than they had had before (John 2.1ff). What are we meant to make of this story in the fourth gospel, and of the other signs that are described in the following chapters of the book?

There must, one thinks, be something equivalent in one's own life, some comparable experience to these signs of glory, so that as we read the gospel we can say to ourselves, It is true, and I know it is true, because the same thing has happened to me. The question is, What is this same thing?

The signs always come in situations of deprivation: a party without wine, a child or an adult who is sick, a crowd that is hungry, disciples who are terrified, a man born blind, Lazarus dead and buried. Glory is revealed in the place where glory is absent, by a miracle.

Are we then to take it that what we are to look for in our lives is miracles that replace our deprivation with plenty, and shame with glory: healings, cures, money suddenly provided out of the blue? This is one way to read the fourth gospel, but I do not believe it is what the author meant to say.

Running through the book from chapter 2 to chapter 12 is a theme that is repeated again and again: Jesus did not trust himself to those who believed in him because they saw the signs that he performed. Nicodemus speaks as an unbeliever when he calls Jesus a rabbi and a teacher sent by God, because of the signs. The signs produce unbelief, and Jesus is put to death because he raised a man from the grave.

The miracle-stories in John prepare us for the crucifixion, and explain it to us. That is the hour, and the miracles are signs that point to its meaning. Jesus gives life, by laying down his life. The glorification is the crucifixion, and the resurrection is the explanation of the death. When Thomas wants a tangible miracle he is rebuked; the blessed are those who believe without seeing.

The glory is in the deprivation, not in the miracle. We are not to look for miracles in our lives, but for the absence of them. Jesus performs miracles in the fourth gospel unwillingly, with protest; they will be misunderstood if we take them to be something other than signs; and the signs point to the glory of not having, of deprivation and emptiness.

The best comment on the signs in the fourth gospel was made (probably before the book was written) by Paul: Power is most fully seen in weakness. I am therefore happy to boast of my weaknesses, because then the power of Christ will rest upon me. So I am content with a life of weakness, insult, hardship, persecution, and distress, all for Christ's sake; for when I am weak, then I am strong (2 Corinthians 12.9f).

THE INVINCIBILITY OF GOD

4th after Epiphany
ASB p.476

THE FUNDAMENTAL CONVICTION of the author of the fourth gospel is that we live in a world that has all been made by one God through his eternal Word. Nothing came into existence except through the Word. John knows that there is darkness, he knows it from experience; but he has no explanation of how it came to be. What he does know is the darkness has never mastered the light, and never shall.

As he writes his story of the light in the world, he shows how it is not understood, not believed, even, in the end, apparently destroyed. Nevertheless, because this is a world made entirely by one God through his Word, nothing can have power over God, his purpose and his love. What happens every time when the darkness attempts to put out the light is the opposite of what was intended: the light shines more brightly. Everything plays into the hands of God, even his opponents. Indeed, his opponents do so more than everybody else.

This is why there is a fundamental optimism in the book: Jesus is lifted up on the cross in order to be destroyed, but the actual result will be that he will draw everybody to him. The intention was to destroy, but the consequence was that he gave life. All the world does go after him.

This fundamental conviction is expressed in the story of Jesus in the temple (2.13ff). The authorities in the temple are the most active opponents of Jesus, as the writer of this gospel explains it. They have no room for the Word who is the life and light of the world, because they serve a system that works without any personal element. (You refuse to come to me . . . 5.40.) Their intention is to preserve the temple by destroying Jesus. Jesus commands them to destroy both him and temple; his zeal for

God's house will cause his destruction. But the result of the death of Jesus is that God raises him to life and that this life is given to all who believe in him. The Father and the Son make their dwelling-place with the humanity they have made; that is the true temple.

All opposition to God is futile, even the opposition that is made in the name of religion. God has not made us in such a way that we can overcome him and defeat his purpose in bringing everything into existence. The love that made everybody will unite everybody to himself; our opposition only has the result of making his glory more apparent, and of enabling him to achieve his goal.

EVERYTHING BELONGS TO YOU

5th after Epiphany
ASB p.480

THE preacher of the gospel is engaged in working for his own redundancy. He is, by the nature of his work, demolishing himself. He saws off the branch he is sitting on, so that he no longer has any special position or status that distinguishes him from everybody else.

This was not so in the Greek philosophical traditions; the names of their founders were passed on and revered. Nor was it so among the Jewish rabbis; they were quoted by name and their followers formed rival groups.

With the disciples of Jesus, however, it should have been different, but it was not. The only wisdom they have is Christ nailed to the cross, an offence to Jews (who believed such a death to be evidence of God's curse on the one who died in that way) and folly to Gentiles (who wanted a different sort of wisdom from that; see 1 Corinthians 1.22–24).

Christianity has bred divisions and sects, and it has to disown its bastard offspring. For us to split into groups headed by a named figure is illegitimate; it is to misunderstand the nature of ministry, and to work on a model that is out of place in the churches.

What is here is greater than Jonah and greater than Solomon (Matthew 12.41f); it is Christ nailed to the cross, and this is God's rejection of every attempt to be wise in a human way, or to be powerful and have influence.

All the traditions of the churches and all their internal tensions and disagreements and schisms of the past, belong to us. We are the heirs of divided Christendom; and we can make what we can of it, except for one thing: we must not use the past to perpetuate divisions into the present and the future.

There is all the difference in the world between owning and being owned. We own the past and are its masters. To take the disagreements of the past and prolong them into the present is to fail to understand who we are and what we are. It is to make human beings and human wisdom into a cause of boasting, and to replace Christ with his agents as though they had some special significance that gave them the authority to continue to cause divisions among Christ's followers. They were not crucified for us.

The wisdom of God rejects any kind of divisive human allegiance, because it is a man nailed to a cross.

GOD'S NO

6th after Epiphany

ASB p.483

IT is a cliché to say that God says Yes to us: welcoming us, accepting us as we are, loving us even though we do not love ourselves. We have heard it all before, many times, and it hardly affects us. What we do not hear so often is that God says No to us: rejecting our proposals and disowning our actions. This Sunday provides an occasion for reflecting our God's refusal to be identified with us.

The gospel is the parable of the wheat and the weeds (Matthew 13.24–30) and central to the parable in the suggestion made by the farmer's employees that they should gather the weeds as soon as they appeared; but he said to them, No. Compare Paul on divisions in Corinth: Pass no premature judgement: wait until the Lord comes. He will bring to light what darkness hides and disclose our inward motives; then will be the time for each to receive commendation from God (1 Corinthians 4.5).

In the gospels, again and again, Jesus says No to the disciples: They are not to send the crowd away (Mark 6.37); John is not to stop the strange exorcist (9.39) and they are not to rebuke those who bring children for Jesus to touch (10.14); the suggestion made by James and John that they should imitate Elijah and call down fire from heaven on the Samaritan villagers is also rejected (Luke 9.54ff).

God will have nothing to do with our zeal for him or with the rigour that we attribute to him, or with the faithlessness that gives up and abandons hope. He is in all respects greater than our ideas about him; if he was not, he would not be God. He rejects our inadequate statements about him; if he did not, he would not be love.

One way to read the history of the church is to see it as the story of God's No to his would-be worshippers; when we are over-zealous and excessively rigorous, he raises up critics and reformers; when we refuse to see what is clearly the case, he blesses those who are outside the church and prospers their research.

To believe in God is to believe in one who is different from our idea of God; in one, that is, who disowns and rejects our well-meant but flawed suggestions.

THE THREE-FOLD CORD

9th before Easter
ASB p.486

THE THEME for this Sunday is Christ the Teacher, an idea that was very congenial to Matthew. He alone of the four evangelists has the passage in which Jesus says to the disciples that they must not be called teacher, because they have only one who is their teacher, and that is Christ (23.10). It is also Matthew alone who arranges the sayings of Jesus in five speeches beginning with the Sermon on the Mount and ending with the warnings of the coming judgement.

But we should notice also that it is Matthew, rather than Mark or Luke, who emphasises the continuing presence of Jesus with his disciples to the end of time (28.20). Those are the last words of Jesus in the book, and they are not to be thought of as cancelled by a later ascension: it is the risen and glorified Lord who is present with them, wherever they meet in his name.

These two themes – the teaching of Jesus in the book, and the presence of Jesus among his followers – present us with a problem: if Matthew has recorded the teaching so fully and arranged it for his readers so systematically, what need is there for the presence of Jesus as the one and only teacher of the church? Matthew must not have thought that the book replaced the Lord, or that the presence of the Lord made it unnecessary to have the book.

There is, however, a further element in Matthew's understanding of this situation. Christ promises to send inspired persons to his church; they are not to be called teachers but they are prophets, wise men and scribes (23.34). Matthew probably saw his own work of revising Mark and enlarging it as a ministry that he had received from the Lord; he was, he would have said, a scribe who had become a learner in the Kingdom of Heaven (13.52). But here again the gifts of God do not cancel one another out; the inspired agent of Christ does not replace the book, nor the book replace the agent; and neither of them displaces the Lord.

As Matthew understands the situation, God deals with the church by means of a three-fold cord: the Lord, who is the only teacher; his agents, who are his mouthpieces and speak his words; the books in which their words (which are Christ's words) are written down.

Matthew states the time when this situation will end, but it is not when Matthew dies, or when the last apostle dies at the close of some 'apostolic age'; the three-fold cord will continue until Christ comes in glory, at the end of time. We still have Christ, his ministers, and their utterances, and our task is to discern his teaching in what they say.

GOD RAISES THE DEAD

8th before Easter
ASB p.490

M ARK shows his readers the meaning of his stories through the way in which he tells them; it is often the apparently unimportant details that we must attend to. When Matthew and Luke came to retell Mark's stories in their own ways, sometimes leaving out the details, they seem to us to have missed Mark's point. It is a fact every small child knows: if the story is told in a different way, it will not do.

Nevertheless, what Matthew and Luke have done has provided us with a method we can follow in reading Mark: look out for what Matthew and Luke have omitted or changed, and that will lead you to see what Mark meant. The story of the paralytic (Mark 2.1ff) is an example.

Neither Matthew nor Luke preserves the detail that those who carried the paralysed man dug up the roof of the house where Jesus was. Matthew has omitted all mention of going up on to the roof (Matthew 9.2ff), and Luke says that they lowered him through the tiles (Luke 5.19). The NEB translation of Mark 2.4, when they had broken through, is literally, when they had dug. What do you think when you hear that four people carried a fifth man on a stretcher, dug a hole and lowered him into it? Doesn't it suggest a funeral? And then the words of Jesus, repeated twice over, Arise, point to resurrection.

The man has been made whole thorough union with Christ in his death and resurrection. We recall what Paul had said to the Romans: Have you forgotten that when we were baptized into union with Christ Jesus we were baptized into his death? By that baptism into his death we were buried with him, in order that, as Christ was raised from the dead by the glorious power of the Father, so also we might set out on a new life (6.3).

33

Baptism is union with Christ in his death and in his resurrection. It sets the pattern by which we live the new life. We are always setting out from the grave of our paralysis and deadness, where we have been with Christ. But we can only arise to the new life if God raises us up.

There was an Old Testament precedent for Mark's story, as is so often the case in his gospel; it is in the account of a dead man thrown into the grave of Elisha: the man came to life and rose to his feet (2 Kings 13.21). Ben Sirach remembered the story and said of Elisha: In life he worked miracles; in death also his deeds were marvellous (Ecclesiasticus 48.14).

The dead Christ is to be found as we reflect on our inability to get anything completely right or do anything wholly good. We touch the dead Christ, as the corpse touched Elisha's bones, and we come to life and rise up through God's power. Like Joseph of Arimathea looking forward to the Kingdom of God (Mark 15.43), we shall find it through the corpse of Jesus.

TO INVITE SINNERS

7th before Easter
ASB p.495

THERE can never be a solution to the problem of Jesus and the church; the problem, that is, of creating an institution (with membership, hierarchy, property and rules) that is compatible with the teaching of Jesus as we find it in the gospels.

Mark's account of the meal after the call of Levi (2.13ff) states the problem, but does nothing to solve it. (The NEB translation, chosen by the compilers of the ASB, is surely unreadable; the REB has made a few improvements.) Those who object to the people who are eating with Jesus are the upholders of the law of Moses, and their attitude is, God has given us rules, so we should observe them; the commandments of God define the people of God. Jesus opposes this; he has invited a tax-collector to follow him, and he has many who do not keep the law among his followers; he says that this is no accident, but his deliberate policy; his purpose was (I came) to invite sinners to God's feast, and his meals were anticipations of the banquet at the end of the world. Fellowship with God is not determined by obedience to God's laws, but by his election and grace; and this will be understood only by those who do not and cannot keep the laws.

A society has to have rules and membership; there must be members and those who are not members; there must be people who have authority to admit and to exclude or eject. All of this is made impossible if the basis of the fellowship is grace and forgiveness.

Philemon found this, to his cost. His duty as a Christian, Paul reminds him, required him to accept as a brother a slave who had absconded and probably defrauded him (1–16). The rules that are necessary for a society have to be broken, and not just the rules of a pagan society; the rules that the church makes for itself must also be ignored if the freedom that Jesus practised is to be the way of life of his followers.

Mark, unlike Matthew, never uses the word 'church' in his gospel; in Mark, Jesus talks about his disciples as 'you'. And what he says is, It shall not be so with you (10.43). What any society, fellowship, organisation or institution must have, is forbidden to the followers of Jesus. This is why there can never be a solution to the problem of Jesus and the church. All we can hope for is an approximation: attempts that will always be unsatisfactory.

LAUGH AT YOURSELF

Ash Wednesday
ASB p.498

JAMES says, in one of today's readings: Be miserable instead of laughing, gloomy instead of happy (4.9); but he would not mind if what we laughed at were ourselves. And this must be what we are meant to do, as we listen to the parable of the two men praying in the temple (Luke 18.9–14).

The parable is a caricature of Pharisees: they were no more prone to self-deception than devoted members of any religious party. The point of the story is not to inform us about Pharisees, which it does not, but about ourselves. And it is not difficult to see how well the cap fits.

We tell God how good we are – thanks to him; we rehearse our success at piety – as if that were what he was interested in; we can be sure of one thing – that we are superior to other people who do not share our taste for religion; while addressing God, we are aware of the person next to us, whom we assess as if we were God.

The pious person is obviously ridiculous, and so are we; religion brings out the bad in us, and makes us laugh at it, and at ourselves. The only hope for us is through that detachment that allow us to stand back and see what we are.

When we were children, our elders used to say, sometimes, when our laughter seemed to them excessive, It will end in tears. Our realization of the foolishness of false piety makes us laugh at ourselves; and the intention is that this laughter should end in tears. The REB translates the passage from James as follows: Turn your laughter into mourning and your gaiety into gloom. If we can hang on long enough, this is how it will be: we shall laugh ourselves out of court, and then ask to come back in, in a more appropriate way. God, have mercy on me, sinner that I am.

HAVE A GOOD LONG LENT

1st in Lent
ASB p.503

SOMEBODY has suggested that Lent is too long; nobody, it is said, can keep up an observance that involves self-discipline for six-and-a-half weeks, so we should settle for less. Passiontide, a fortnight, perhaps; or Holy Week; or the old traditional three days, or just an Easter Vigil, and call it a day. The question is, however, whether there is something about time, and our experience of duration, that cannot be replaced by anything.

The author of the Letter to the Hebrews had seen the point: the Son of God had to be made like us in every way, so that he might be our high priest before God (2.17). He had to learn what it is like to live in time, with before and after, now and not yet. There was no other way in which he could know what it feels like to be a creature of time such as we are, and represent us before God, except by becoming one himself. That was what this writer thought.

There are things that can only be experienced in time – it would be impossible to explain what it is like to wait for something to happen to a person who had had no experience of duration; just as it must be impossible to explain colour to someone who has never seen anything. Anyone brought up with everything always to hand has missed out on a large area of experience that others, not brought up in this way, have had.

It would be an entirely different exercise to keep a shorter Lent; it might be very good, but it would be different; it would have different results. A long Lent requires more than a short burst of enthusiasm; it requires endurance when the enthusiasm that was there at the beginning has run out; it requires patience with oneself, when discipline fails.

Anyone who has taken part in a retreat of two or three days, or more, knows that the experience of it is dependent on the length of time involved. People who have spent a day of silent prayer together, or a night vigil, or a Good Friday Three Hours' service, know that the length of the operation is what makes it what it is. There is no way of avoiding length of time, and no substitute for it.

It is the same with prayer. It cannot be rushed; and it cannot be compressed into a shorter time. There are common sayings that express the idea: it takes time; give it time. Learn to wait. Don't think you can hurry it up.

Whatever we think about it, it is the case that we are creatures of time, and we live in it. We have to learn to use it wisely. There are lessons about ourselves and about God and the way things are that it will take time for us to learn. Patience and endurance can only be experienced over a considerable length of time. Six-and-a-half weeks is not too long for this purpose.

HE CRIES FOR US

2nd in Lent
ASB p.508

THERE are only two places in the gospels where Jesus is said to have wept: at the tomb of Lazarus in the fourth gospel, where the cause of his tears is the unbelief of Mary and Martha and their friends; and in today's gospel (Luke 19.41–48), where he sees Jerusalem and foresees the disaster that awaits it.

We do not find the picture of the weeping Christ attractive. It is not English for men to cry; only women do that. Men should conceal their emotions, we think; or, better still, not have them. We are embarrassed.

There is more to it, though, than that. What we really resent is that anyone should weep for us. The two passages, in John and in Luke, are there because the evangelists believed that they were telling their readers what the attitude of Jesus was to them: he weeps for our blindness and our folly; we do not know what we are doing and we cannot foresee what will be the consequences of our actions. We are meant to say to ourselves: Jesus weeps for us as late-20th-century Europeans and as members of the Church of England; we are about to reap the harvest of our past mistakes in all the spheres of our life. The question is, Can we do this?

If we are to do it, what we shall need to see is that, in spite of all the embarrassment, there is good news here. All we have to do is to allow ourselves to look and to make sure that we see. We must accept that, for all we dislike it, we are people for whom somebody is weeping.

It will need determination and courage for this to happen. It would be easier and more pleasant to think of something else. We shall have to accept that we are not the nice people we thought we were who cause no pain to others and never harm anybody. On the contrary, we are those who make Christ cry. He cries because of our blindness and because of our inability to do anything about it. He cries: but at least he is not angry with us. And he has not finished with us yet. You do not weep for those you hate, but those you love. He weeps while he is on the way to Jerusalem to die. His tears are good news, because he will die for those for whom he has cried.

JESUS HAD TO DIE

3rd in Lent
ASB p.512

TODAY's gospel (Luke 9.18–27) includes the first of the predictions of the passion and resurrection. Jesus says that the Son of Man is destined to suffer grievously, to be rejected, to be put to death and to be raised up. These are things which he says must happen.

If we had asked the Christians in the early centuries why these things had to be, the first answer they would have given us would have been: Because these events were foretold in scripture. We can see that this was what they believed, from the way in which they tell the story of the passion; the echoes of the prophets and the psalms leave us in no doubt that what had happened was, they believed, what God had announced beforehand in scripture. Christ died for our sins according to the scriptures.

That answer, however, would have left us asking another question. Then tell us, we should have said, why it was foretold? Can you not give us another reason why these things had to be ? Because, to be honest with you, we do not find your use of prophecy convincing.

They had another explanation of why it was necessary for Christ to be rejected, put to death and raised to life, and they would not have minded our asking them for it. It was, in fact, already built in to the earliest version of the events, in Mark's gospel. That oldest account of the passion of Christ did not let anyone off the hook: the Jews and the Romans; Judas, the ten, then Peter (specially Peter: three times for him) – all reject him; even the women are at a distance (My friends and companions shun me in my sickness, and my kinsfolk keep far off – Psalm 38.11), and in the end they say nothing to anybody, because they are afraid.

Nobody at all was left in a position to say, I stood by him; I did not fail him; he did not need to die for me, because I was willing to die for him. The first writers of the passion thought that everybody, Jews and gentiles, religious and irreligious, righteous and sinners, were all in need of what Christ could give them, and that he could only give it to them after he had been rejected and put to death.

The Christ who accepts us and welcomes us and gives us all his gifts is the Christ whom we have handed over to destruction; he is the one who loves us and gives himself up for us. The necessity for his dying and rising lies in us: he could find no better way of entering our lives than as the one whom we had destroyed.

FREE FOR ALL

4th in Lent
ASB p.517

THERE IS a certain sort of person who is always telling us that our problem is that we do not believe in ourselves. We know what they mean and recognize that it is true, though we might not have put it quite like that; we thought it was God we had to believe in, not ourselves.

But it is certainly true that believing in God has, as one of its consequences, believing in yourself. Paul says it, for example, in the passage from 2 Corinthians (3.4–18) that is one of this Sunday's readings: he does not do what Moses did; Moses concealed the glory of his face as he came down from the mountain with the law, but Paul does not do that as he comes with the gospel; he lets the glory be seen.

Paul is no different in this respect from any other Christian believer. All of us reflect the glory of the Lord with uncovered faces. (The ASB uses the TEV translation; for a different way of understanding the Greek word, see REB. Nevertheless, the idea is certainly there in the passage as a whole: What Moses concealed, we are very bold and we reveal.)

What are we to make of this? Are other people seeing a special light coming out of the back of my head? Ought I to see it in others? Or is this not what Paul means? He gives us a hint to follow up and explain the meaning of glory when he says: Where the Spirit of the Lord is present, there is freedom. Belief in God, and thus in ourselves as his agents, is to express itself in the freedom we have in Christ.

We are free from all kinds of law: superstition, ambition, compulsion, fear, convention, slavery of every kind, immaturity and so on. We are no longer tied and bound, but we are set free to do the most extraordinary things that will surprise other people and ourselves. We can say things that we never thought we could get our tongues round; we can speak the truth in love; we can meet people whose company we dreaded; we can touch and handle anything. This is the glorious freedom of the children of God, and we have it now and already.

What we are to believe about ourselves is that we can face anything through him who gives us strength.

THE JOKE IS ON HIM

5th in Lent
ASB p.521

THE PROBLEM WAS (to speak in a very human way), How could God make an entrance into our lives? The difficulty was not on his side, but all on ours; we did so resist him; we were suspicious and self-willed. Maybe we had to be, to survive;

maybe God had deliberately made us like that. Suppose, then, that God were to come to us as a human being: a baby, a fellow penitent presenting himself alongside us for John to baptize; a teacher and a charismatic healer; one through whom the light and glory of God shone, for disciples to see – would that get round our resistance? No, we should still be suspicious and unwilling to open the door and let him in.

There was one way left. He would have to become a has-been; one who no longer had life or power to dominate us, as we thought; then we would not feel threatened by him. The gift that God has to give us, which is himself, is not ready and prepared for us until Jesus has died; only then can it be said, It is finished. Death makes it complete; it wraps it up for us. Because now there is no power, no majesty, no goodness, to make us feel threatened and inferior. A living dog is better than a dead lion: the lion, then, must die. And unless a wheat grain falls into the ground and dies, it remains a single grain (John 12.24, this Sunday's gospel). The clever hostess makes every guest feel welcome. Even the shyest lose all fear, because she makes them feel wanted. They can even manage to talk to the other guests, because she has coped with them: she gives them the confidence they need.

But in order to do this, she will have to have removed all the barriers timidity and suspicion can erect; she will have to have divested herself of what it is that might be frightening about her – what it is that makes her different. Perhaps she does it by her humour; if so, it is because she is the butt of her jokes; her humour is turned against herself.

Paul said to the Corinthians, We proclaim Christ nailed to the cross; and to the Galatians, Jesus Christ was openly displayed on the cross. This is the way in which God comes to our door in order to enter our lives: as one who has just breathed his last. The joke is entirely on him; but by coming this way, he has got through our barrier of fear and suspicion; we cannot now feel unwanted.

HE DENIED HIMSELF

Palm Sunday
ASB p.526

IN MARK'S GOSPEL, Jesus tells the disciples to follow him and then shows them, in the passion narrative (Mark 14.32–15.41), what they must do. They must disown themselves, he says (8.34), and we wonder what that means; but when we read the account of the trials and of the crucifixion itself, we find out. He did not deny that he was the Christ, the Son of the Blessed; when the high priest put the question to him, he answered, I am. After that, however, he made no further statement in reply to the charges made against him, and Mark draws our attention to this silence of Jesus, by saying that Pilate was astonished.

To deny oneself, then, is not to be dishonest; it is to own up to who you are. (This is what Peter does not do.) But then, after that, it is to make no further statement; to refrain from threats and warnings. There is a contrast here between Jesus and Jeremiah; Jeremiah had said, You may be certain that, if you put me to death, you and this city and those who live in it will be guilty of murdering an innocent man; for it was the Lord who sent me to you to say all this to you (26.15). Jesus says nothing of that sort. Instead, he made himself nothing, in his silence, and allowed himself to be destroyed. He did not try to save his life. He practised what he had told all who wanted to be his followers they should do.

This was the only way in which he could be the one who saved others; it had to be through not attempting to save himself, specially by means of threats and warnings of the consequences that would follow. How could we possibly approach him as the one who gave his life as a ransom for many, if he had uttered curses on his killers, or said anything to make us fear him? His determination to deny himself is the necessary ground of our faith in him as the saviour.

MY BODY IS FOR YOU

Maundy Thursday
ASB p.552

WHEN I was hungry, you gave me food; when thirsty, you gave me drink. You put these first on the list of good works, before shelter and clothing; we should die of starvation before we died of exposure. Knowing our need, you provide for it; giving us what we most urgently require.

But what you give is not what we expected, but the broken piece of a loaf and drink from a common cup. This food and drink will not take the place of all our other meals. What will it do?

You say it is your body and your blood; that what you give us is yourself; you give us yourself, in order that we may live, and you do it on this day of your death, in the night of your arrest. What is to happen to you is being done for us.

We know how we depend on other people, and could scarcely live without them: our parents, teachers, colleagues; those who cope with our problems; those who perform routine jobs at unsocial hours; our friends and our neighbours. It is no problem to think of someone doing for us what we cannot do for ourselves.

We live off other people, much as we live off our food; they give themselves to us, and are diminished by our existence. And at the centre of this interaction of giving and receiving, you take your place as the one who gives himself completely, to everybody.

HE DIED FOR US

Good Friday
ASB p.558

THE meaning of the crucifixion and the resurrection is all there in the account of what happened; it is not as though we had to have further information to make sense of it. Jesus had proclaimed God's coming kingdom and associated people with him on the understanding that he and they together would be members of God's new world, when the time came. They were to follow him, and he expected trouble and persecution.

They went to Jerusalem together, and he was arrested, but they avoided arrest and escaped – one without his clothes; Peter by disowning him. There is no doubt that none of the disciples was crucified with Jesus, though they believed afterwards that they should have been; he had invited them to take up their cross.

There was every reason for Jesus to have written them off, and they would have had no excuse if he had. But here again there is a fact of which we can be certain: they believed that he had appeared to them, alive, after his death and burial; and that he had not disowned them, but commissioned them to preach his death and resurrection.

We know that within a short time they were saying:

He died for our sins, in accordance with the scriptures;
   he was buried;
   he was raised to life on the third day, in accordance with the scriptures;
   he appeared to Cephas (Peter)
(1 Corinthians 15.3ff)

His death had been for their benefit, to deal with all their

46

failures and disobedience to God. And it had been God's intention that it should be so – that was what they meant when they said it was in accordance with the scriptures.

Therefore they were not to think that their desertion of Jesus was the end of his relationship with them; it was the beginning of a new relationship, in which their weakness was dealt with by God's goodness: He died for their sins, to make something of them, to cope with what they were.

This is why we call it Good Friday.

JOY AND REJOICING

Easter Day
ASB p.573

EASTER DAY demands that we change our attitude, from the long weeks of Lenten penitence, to joy and rejoicing; and to do this is not easy, nor does it come naturally. For many of us, there is less effort required in being sad and depressed, than in being joyful. It comes to us more easily to weep with those who weep, than to rejoice with those who rejoice.

Rejoicing, which is appropriate for Easter Day, needs faith to set it in motion, specially in a bleak world of hunger, disease and violence. What is there to be joyful about? Christ's resurrection, the reason for joy, seems irrelevant.

There is no problem about being miserable on your own; it is not so easy to rejoice on your own. The natural thing is to call together your friends and neighbours and say, Rejoice with me. Joy is social: unhappiness tends to isolate us.

How wise, then, of our ancestors to say that 'Every Parishioner shall communicate at the least three times in the year, of which Easter to be one'. The service, the readings, the presence of other people, the whole occasion, draws us out from the privacy of depression and misery into a new world of joy. We had forgotten that it was there, but the day calls it to mind and plunges us into it again:

> Deck thyself, my soul, with gladness,
> Leave the gloomy haunts of sadness,
> Come into the daylight's splendour,
> There with joy thy praises render
> Unto him whose grace unbounded
> Hath this wondrous banquet founded;
> High o'er all the heavens he reigneth,
> Yet to dwell with thee he deigneth.

SURPRISED BY FAITH

1st after Easter
ASB p.602

SHOULD Thomas have asked for proof of Christ's resurrection, in today's gospel (John 20.19–29), or was he wrong to say what he did? Are the words of Jesus meant to be a rebuke to Thomas, or simply a question of fact? – Have you believed because you have seen me? Blessed are those who have not seen and yet believe. The whole story can be read in two ways, and has been. But it may be that it does not matter which way we take it, because neither affects the point. The point of the story is that Christ is not restricted by the conditions laid down by Thomas; in the end, Thomas does believe (My Lord and my God!) without putting his finger into the place where the nails were, or his hand into the Lord's side. God gets round our unbelief, and our belief, too. He is not thwarted by us, and cannot be.

The thought might occur to us that the church and Christianity are coming to an end; that we have all outgrown the need for any religion. Our requirements are such, we might think, that faith in a God of any kind is impossible and unnecessary. The Thomas story provides no support for such an idea. We cannot exclude the possibility of our believing by laying down conditions in advance; or of anyone else believing.

Faith is a strange thing; it turns up unexpectedly, in the most unlikely places. You can easily see how people thought it was a gift from God. It comes from his side, not from ours. Nobody thinks himself into it. Rightly or wrongly, Thomas supposed that he would not be a believer, unless . . . But he did believe, without the fulfilment of his conditions. God is greater than our heart.

GOD'S HALLMARK

2nd after Easter
ASB p.607

LUKE DOES NOT EXPLAIN how the breaking of the bread was the moment at which Cleopas and his companion recognized Jesus (Luke 24. 13–35). It has been suggested that it was something to do with the way that Jesus performed the action; or that it was simply the fact that Jesus did what would normally be done by the host, not by a guest. Cleopas was not one of the apostles; and so, one assumes, he was not present at the Last Supper, when Jesus broke the bread and said, This is my body (Luke 22.19).

But perhaps this is all to ask more of Luke than we should. It is often possible to pick holes in his stories. He has left us to work it out for ourselves. Jesus, we remember, gave the disciples his body at the supper before he was arrested, passing them the bread. He meant that all he was going to do, he was going to do for them; they would be the beneficiaries of his coming death and resurrection. Now, before he ascends to heaven to send the Spirit to his followers, he again breaks bread and offers it to them. He is expressing himself in the same way.

God is the one who gives us all good things: the world, our life, and all that is excellent. Jesus is of God, and he too is a giver: breaking bread and giving it is his hallmark. They exist for us, and we exist through them. The symbolic action says it all.

IT IS THE LORD

3rd after Easter
ASB p.612

THE STORY of the miraculous catch of fish (John 21.1–14) is also a story of how Jesus revealed himself to his disciples. At the beginning of the paragraph, none of the disciples knows who it is who is standing on the beach and speaking to them. The first person to recognize him is the disciple whom Jesus loved; he says to Peter, It is the Lord. In the end, none of them dared to ask him who he was, because they all knew it was the Lord. Then comes the conclusion: this was now the third time that Jesus was revealed to the disciples after he was raised from the dead.

The story encourages those who hear it to look to their own situation and learn to say of what happens there, It is the Lord. He is still the one who has all authority in heaven and on earth.

We are to recognize him as we reflect on what is happening around us. We continue the tradition that goes back to Eli (It is the Lord: let him do what seemeth him good: 1 Samuel 3.18) and to Job (The Lord gave, and the Lord hath taken away; blessed be the name of the Lord: Job 1.21).

This may sound very pietistical; but in fact what we have here is a highly critical tool. We are required to distinguish between what is of the Lord, and what is only a passing fashion or a bright idea. It would be a mistake of the worst kind to endorse everything that happened with: It is the Lord. We have to discriminate; to test the spirits; to keep hold of what is good, and reject everything else.

The church is meant to be a body of people who can discriminate between what is good and what is not. In the story in John 21, one disciple realizes who the stranger is, before the others; but in the end, they all know. And this is how it often is in the church, too. There are those who have greater insight and can see what the Lord is doing; they help the rest of us to understand.

GENUINE GOODS AND FAKES

4th after Easter
ASB p.617

IT IS A PITY that the Revelation is probably the book that is least read and least understood by Christian people in the West today, because a good case can be made for the view that, of all the New Testament writings, it is the one we need most. We need it because it offers us a way of looking at what is going on all around us and of understanding it. John believes we are in the middle of a war, and that we are on one side or the other; it would be a fatal mistake to think you were a neutral. The opponents are Jerusalem and Babylon, truth and the lie. Each side claims our allegiance and offers us its own rewards; those of Babylon have an obvious attraction, whereas those of Jerusalem are not so instantly appealing.

Babylon deals in consumer goods; its leading citizens are traders, and their goods are all catalogued in chapter 18; notice particularly that slaves and human lives come at the bottom of the list. The rewards of Jerusalem are of an entirely different class from this: The throne of God and of the Lamb will be there, and his servants shall worship him; they shall see him face to face and bear his name on their foreheads (22.3f.).

It is John's central conviction that the rewards of Babylon are all illusory; they are fakes that do not satisfy and they will all be destroyed. The readers and hearers of the book are meant to join in the great shout of Hallelujah! that comes in chapter 19, when they hear that Babylon (which stands for the Roman Empire, and any other consumer society) is to be destroyed for ever. Jerusalem, on the other hand, will remain, and her rewards are the only genuine joys that will give the satisfaction that they promise.

John expects his readers to die in the war; and this dying he calls conquering. The Lord who had appeared to him and inspired him to write the book had been victorious in his death, and now he invites the readers to die with him in the war between Jerusalem and Babylon, the Empire and the churches, consumerism and spirituality. He who conquers, I will grant him to sit with me on my throne, as I myself conquered and sat down with my Father on his throne (Revelation 3.21).

DEFEAT AND VICTORY

5th after Easter
ASB p.622

JOHN (THE EVANGELIST), like Mark before him, makes use of the mistakes and misunderstandings of the disciples as one of the ways by which the readers of his gospel can come to the truth (John 16.25-end). The disciples think that Jesus knows everything and that he reveals it all in words; that he is a messenger come from God. But this is not what is to be believed. John believes that Jesus reveals the Father in his actions even more than in his words. (I shall tell you of the Father in plain words, is probably a mistranslation; I shall ... tell you plainly, or publicly, is what is meant; not in words, but by his death and resurrection.) The truth is not something to be spoken; Jesus is the truth, and to have it they must have him (see 1 John 5.12).

John expects his readers to be able to see one thing in and through another; if they cannot do this, they will miss what has been done for them. They are going to be persecuted, for example; the world will reject them, as it rejected Jesus. But if they cannot see further than that, they will not know the peace that they do in fact have, a peace that is not threatened or destroyed by being persecuted. The world's rejection of Jesus was far more than simply that: it was Jesus's victory over the world; his laying down his life was his conquest of the world. He gave the life that he had received and he took it again to give to all whom he draws to himself by his exaltation on the cross. His death was not failure, but success; victory, not defeat.

In the same way, they might think that Jesus was alone and deserted during the crucifixion. Zechariah had said, Strike the shepherd, and the sheep will be scattered (13.7); the verse had been quoted in Mark (15.27), and the last words of Jesus in that gospel had been: My God, my God, why have you forsaken me? (14.34). But John wants his readers to see more than that.

53

The Father was with the Son, because the Son was obeying the Father's command.

Jesus says that he is leaving the world and going to the Father. If the disciples think that this is plain speaking they are completely mistaken. How could they abide in him, as he has told them they must (chapter 15), if he were not with them still, while they continue to be in the world?

In the fourth gospel, nothing is what it seems; there is always more than what appears to be the case. John believes that this is true of the Christian life, also; and that may be why he writes in this complicated way. Peace and joy are compatible with trouble; there is one who is with us in spite of (because of?) his apparent absence. Faith changes the signs, making positives out of negatives, and negatives out of positives.

WHERE IS JESUS NOW?

Ascension Day
ASB p.627

WHEN Christians of the first century said that Jesus had been raised from the dead, they found that they had a question that followed on from this belief: If Jesus is alive, where is he now? The answer was not simple; in fact, there were four answers, and each of the four evangelists favoured one of them.

Mark, the earliest, presents Jesus as the one who will come to gather his chosen from all over the earth; they are to be ready for him; like the door-keeper whose sole purpose is to be ready for the master of the house on his return. The final speech of Jesus in Mark's gospel, ends with this instruction: What I say to you, I say to everyone: keep awake (Mark 13.37).

Matthew moves the reader's attention from the future coming (which is still there in his book) to the presence of Jesus with the disciples till the end of time. When two or three meet together in his name, he is there among them (Matthew 18.20). The congregation assembles, Matthew's book is read to them, and faith receives the promise that what Jesus had said and done and suffered in the past, he continues to say and do and suffer in the present.

Luke stresses a different aspect of Christian belief. He alone has an account of the departure of Jesus from his disciples, at the end of the gospel and at the beginning of Acts. He asserts the approval that Jesus had received from God who raised him from the dead and exalted him to sit at his right hand. The ascension is the Father's assurance that what Jesus had said was true.

The fourth evangelist presents yet another aspect: he never says that Jesus went away from the disciples, after the resurrection; rather, he came to them, and remains with them; he is the vine, and they are the branches; the Father and the Son make their dwelling-place with the one who loves him; Christ abides in the believer, and the believer abides in Christ.

Where is Jesus now? They said: He is coming; he is with us when we meet; he is with God; he is in me. What was believed needed to be expressed in different ways that might seem contradictory and incompatible, but were necessary if one were to attempt to do justice to all that had to be said.

ASCENSION JOY

Sunday after Ascension Day
ASB p.629

THE DISCIPLES went back to Jerusalem from the place near Bethany where Jesus ascended into heaven, with great joy, Luke says in today's gospel (24.45-end). One might well be surprised at this; would you not expect sorrow rather than joy at a time of departure and separation? It is Luke, and only Luke of all the New Testament writers, who has an account of the ascension into heaven as a separate act of God on a particular day (Acts 1.3); and there is nothing either in his gospel or in Acts to suggest that Jesus is present with disciples between that day and the time when he will come again as the judge of the world. The Spirit is given to take the place of Jesus. So why does Luke say that there was joy at the departure of Jesus?

The way Luke saw it was like this: the ascension was the final evidence that Jesus had been right all along, in everything he had said and done. The resurrection and the ascension were ways in which God endorsed what Jesus had said. He had preached repentance and promised forgiveness and justification to those who confessed their sins; he had eaten and drunk with tax-collectors and sinners; and he had been put to death for it. Who was right, those who put him to death, or he and his followers who would continue to preach repentance for the forgiveness of sins, in his name (that is, on his authority) to all nations? God's exaltation of Jesus to his right hand was the seal of God's approval of him; that was why Luke made so much of it. When the apostles preached Jesus and the resurrection, they were preaching forgiveness for those who repented and were baptised, on the authority of Jesus.

The joy of the disciples after the ascension is therefore the joy of those who now know that God has forgiven them and accepted them, as Jesus said he would. Christianity according to Luke is

God-centred, not Jesus-centred; it is expressed in praise of God, not in the form of love for Jesus. Hence Luke's last words in his gospel, which match the beginning of the book: They were continually in the temple praising God.

It is important to recognize the differences between the writers of the New Testament. They show that there are more ways than one of understanding Christianity. There are the differences between the four evangelists, and between them and Paul, John of the Revelation, the writer of Hebrews, and so on. We are different from one another, and our way of believing will be different from that of others. It has always been so; God must love differences. It would be a mistake to iron them out.

These differences, however, do not divide us from one another. Luke, like Paul, John and the others, believed that joy was an essential mark of a believer. Its absence would be a sign that something had gone wrong.

THE PLACE OF JESUS

Pentecost
ASB p.634

WHAT THE SPIRIT DOES, according to today's gospel (John 14.15–26) is make us understand what we should not otherwise have known. On that day (when the Spirit is given) you will understand that I am in my Father and you in me and I in you. What will be understood then is expressed here in terms of place, and the word that is used must be one of the simplest and commonest in any language; it is the short word 'in'. We are promised that we shall know that the Son is in the Father, and that we are in the Son and that the Son is in us. If we could find out what John means by 'in' we should know what it is that

57

the Spirit does. He makes it possible for us to see the inwardness of the situation; but what does that mean?

We have a similar idiom in English. We say: I know that man's face but I cannot place him. To place him, if we could do it, would be to know who he is, what he does, how we were involved with him in the past, and under what conditions we might find ourselves meeting him again.

The Spirit, John means, is the way in which we are able to place Jesus – and ourselves. We shall see that he is the agent of the Father, the one by whom God deals with his creation and gives it his final and greatest gift. We shall also see that what we have received is the gift of God's own existence; he has shared his life with us, through the Son who is our life. The place of Jesus is in God; he is also in us; and our place is in him.

The Spirit is spoken of here as light which illuminates the mind and shows the truth of the situation. Other evidence, taken by itself, would be far too thin for anyone to build anything on it. How could we possibly think that we shared God's life? What sort of facts could lead us to think that we are gods (John 10.34f)? This is the way the deranged speak. John's understanding of what Jesus is and what believers are is so exalted that nothing less than God's Spirit is needed to make them able to know and accept the high claims that he makes for him and for them.

THREE-FOLD LOVE

Trinity Sunday
ASB p.640

O NE WAY to think about the world is to suppose that God has put a distance between him and it, and withdrawn to let it be itself; he does not interfere with its running, but allows events to take their course; this is why there are accidents and disasters.

That may be all right for some days, but on Trinity Sunday we need a different way of looking at the world. God is not to be thought of as one who has withdrawn, but he gives his whole attention to what he has made. Take anything you like, however small and apparently insignificant, and it is the object of God's three-fold love.

Simply because it exists, it is his by being there, because he is the maker of everything, seen and unseen. It is there because he wanted it to be. The fact of its existence, which makes it possible for us to think about it, is the result of God's will. There is no other maker than he. Anything there is, might not be; but it is. And the reason why it is, is because God wanted it to exist. It is, because he loves it.

There is more to it than that. As well as being the maker, he is also the saviour. Nothing is quite right; everything is crumbling, ageing and disappearing. But it will not be so always. The maker is also the redeemer, and he will make perfect what looks and is a most imperfect world. Nothing is outside the scope of his purpose; he would not have made it, if it had been.

There is even more than that. What we have is only a world of emptinesses: everything is hollow and porous and desiccated, and what it needs is filling. God will do that, too. The Holy Spirit is God pouring himself out into what he both makes and mends. We do not know what the end of it will be; only that God will be all, in all.

Trinity Sunday encourages us to indulge in a kind of pathetic fallacy: that it is the same for animals and vegetables and minerals as it is for us. Trinity Sunday does not encourage us to think that God is only concerned with human beings. The difference between us and the rest of the creation is that we know what it is like to experience being the objects of trinitarian love: being here, and in need of redirection, and longing to be filled and completed. We generalize from what we know about ourselves, without having a clear idea what it means: he makes everything, saves it and fulfils it; what he is to us, he is to all his creatures.

DELIGHT IN DEPENDENCE

2nd after Pentecost
ASB p.643

PERPAPS one of the things that will surprise us most, when we eventually see ourselves as God sees us (or even as others see us), is the extent to which we have been dependent on other people. We thought we were unique, original, the inventors of ourselves; what we shall see is how little we made up and how much we borrowed, without acknowledgement. We are all plagiarists.

Sometimes, even now, you catch yourself out at it. You reread a book that you have not opened for years, and there hits you from the page an idea that you have repeated so often that you thought it was your own: so that is where it came from; I did not invent it. (I confess, to my shame, that I even described something once as Fenton's Law, and then found it, in the identical words, in a book by C.S. Lewis that I had read and for-gotten.)

We are not original; we stand on the shoulders of our predeces-sors. (Even that may be to express it too optimistically: better to say, we hang on to their coat-tails.) And we are still more derivative than that.

We could not talk or think without the vocabulary we inherited, and the syntax, and many of the ready-made sentences that we repeat. And there is more to life than thinking and talking; there are assumptions about what is right and what is wrong, and they also were fed into us at some point. I found myself explaining to an American student the other day that I had been brought up in such a way that I would be embarrassed if I were to be seen eating in the street; she had no such inhibitions, and found my attitude quaint. But there is still more.

We have good desires, from time to time; we even bring some of them to good effect. Where do they come from, and how do we get the grace to fulfil them? Have we thought enough about the fact that we are being prayed for? Every church service includes some petition for God to be with us all, evermore; or for the whole state of Christ's church; or for all, according to their need. We are being upheld, all the time, by other people, who put their goodwill into intercession for everybody, and that includes us. One day, we shall see it. The good works that I did (and felt rather pleased with) were not much mine; I borrowed the power to do them, and the idea of doing them, from the goodwill of others.

We grow up in a society, and draw on it. We are redeemed in a society, and we draw on it, too. The degree to which we are debtors to others will astonish and eventually delight us.

MY JOY AND YOUR JOY

3rd after Pentecost
ASB p.648

W HY does Jesus say, in today's gospel (John 15.11) that his own joy will be in us, and our joy will be complete? It looks as though he means that our joy will not be complete unless his joy is in us. What is the relation between the joy of another person and one's own?

There certainly seem to be some occasions on which other people's joy affects us deeply; one thinks of the wedding of a friend, or someone's success in an exam, or promotion. Whatever it is that makes them happy makes us happy too; their joy is our joy. And if it is not, we suspect that there is something wrong with us, and we look carefully for jealousy, envy, malice and all the other negative attitudes that must be blocking us from sharing another's happiness.

It may be that joy is all the more pure and intense when it is not ours, but derived from another person. When it is derived, we did nothing to contribute to it; we simply experienced it as the overflowing of our neighbour's joy; we shared it without having done anything to deserve it or to make it happen. It was pure gift.

The Baptist, in John's gospel, compares himself to the bridegroom's friend, who stands by and listens to him and is overjoyed at hearing the bridegroom's voice. He adds: This is my joy and now it is complete (3.29).

Christ's joy is the result of his keeping the Father's commandments and remaining in his love. He lays down his life for his friends, and that is the reason for his joy. He passes this joy on to us, and it makes our joy complete as we also keep his commandments and remain in his love, laying down our lives for the brethren.

We cannot have joy in isolation from others. We cannot, either, pursue it as an end. It is a gift to be received, not a goal to be sought. If it is to be complete, it must be somebody else's joy, experienced as undeserved and unmerited: we are revellers at Christ's party, louts who have nothing of their own to shout about, but who still shout.

GOD'S ADULT FAMILY

4th after Pentecost
ASB p.653

ONE OF THE FIRST mistakes that Christians made was to fail to see that they were free. They were like Peter in prison in Acts: they did not think that they had really been released but imagined that it was just a dream (12.9). The first heresy was to think that there were still religious rules that had to be kept.

Paul's gentile converts in Galatia wanted to keep the Jewish law: they wanted to submit to rules that would abolish their freedom. If they were to accept the law, they would have to avoid certain activities on Saturdays, abstain from certain kinds of food, and perform irrational ceremonies such as circumcision. Paul is horrified, and he writes the Letter to the Galatians to say so.

We read the Letter, but what they did does not immediately horrify us. We are used to Christians keeping rules; we even keep them ourselves. One of the ways we experience Christianity most powerfully is as a negative force, forbidding us to do certain things that we find attractive and would certainly do if they were not ruled out by our faith, we think. The negative is more prominent than the positive; what is forbidden is clearer than what we are free to do; we listen more closely to those who tell us what we should not do, than to those who tell us that God has released us from the prison of rules and set us at liberty; we find it hard to believe that we are adults before God, and would rather stand before him as children. The true Christian position, according to Paul, is that God has abolished the rules and set us free to do anything except sin; and that is no real exception, since sin is a kind of non-event, a failure to love, missing the mark.

If I ask myself the question, Is it all right for me to do this? then the presumption is, Yes, it is all right. The only thing that is forbidden is not to love. Our only problem is to accept our freedom from taboos and restrictions that make life easier for us. We love our prisons, and want to get back to them as soon as possible. Paul's letter is all about the deceitful attractiveness of religious rules that restrict the freedom of the grown-up family of God.

NO TO THE RICH

5th after Pentecost
ASB p.658

NO ONE planning to preach on the gospel appointed for this Sunday, the rich man (Matthew 19.16–26), will need me or anybody else to warn them of the dangers that lie in wait. Every preacher knows from past experience that voluntary poverty is not yet the way in which the majority of the members of the Church of England see their vocation; and that the subject arouses anger and ill will whenever it is raised. After 1900 years, Christianity may have made fornication and indecency (REB, vice) shameful, but it has not yet succeeded, at least in England, in doing the same for the greed which makes an idol of gain (Ephesians 5.5, part of today's epistle). We drool enviously over lists of rich people.

What we must expect is to be told that Jesus said, Sell your possessions, and give to the poor, to only one person in the gospels, not to all; that it was only if he wished to go the whole way that he had to do this; that by a camel, Jesus meant a rope; that the needle's eye was the name of a gate, and you could get a camel through it; that Jesus and his disciples lived in a different kind of society (and climate) from ours, so that what he said does not apply to us.

Most, if not all, of these suggestions are not true. They are all ways of avoiding the offensive saying of Jesus that, as a commentator put it: 'The entrance of a rich person into the kingdom turns out to be, not nearly impossible, not even fully impossible, but more than impossible' (R.H. Gundry, *Mark*, 1993).

The disciples were amazed to hear this, as one might have expected. There is no reason why we should try to make it acceptable, to ourselves or to other people. All the evidence is that Jesus was a difficult person, who did not fit in; his contemporaries (with the one exception of Peter) did nothing to prevent him from being executed by the Romans. His message included the insight that to enter the kingdom you must give up everything, with joy. God cannot be loved alongside other things.

It is a message easy enough to understand and consent to; the only problem is carrying it out. All greed that makes an idol of gain must go. We must say it as clearly as possible, and hope to put it into practice; there will be offence; and we shall have to admit that our own performance is woefully inadequate.

GOD'S JOY

6th after Pentecost
ASB p.663

IN TODAY'S GOSPEL, the parable of the Prodigal Son (Luke 15.11-end), two characters look at the same situation from different points of view, and see it, therefore, in different ways. The father rejoices at the return of one of his sons; the older brother regards the boy as a mere wastrel, who has destroyed part of the family wealth. We are meant to choose between the two.

People who have never heard the story before (there are more of them around now than there used to be) and do not know in advance what the evangelist expects them to think, often agree with the older brother, not with the father. The younger son, they think, was a drop-out, and it was silly of the old man to make such a fuss of him; in any case, the fatted calf was now the property of the older brother, so the father had no right to have it slaughtered. It is an understandable point of view. The father, on the other hand, appeals to something more than what is understandable and straight-forward: he appeals to necessity.

The Greek that the RSV translates 'it was fitting' (*edei*) means 'it had to be'; REB has: 'How could we fail to celebrate this happy day?' The father can see the necessity, the older brother cannot; the reason why the father can see it is because he is the boy's father, and the one who has come home is his son.

What the older brother needs to do is read the earlier part of the chapter in which he is a character: if he had lost one of his sheep and found it, he would rejoice; if he had lost one of his coins and found it, he would rejoice. The father is doing the same thing as the sheep-owner and the woman; hence the repetition of the saying that the lost has been found (verses 6,9,32). The epistle (Colossians 3.12–17) is about putting on a new set of attitudes, as if they were clean clothes: compassion, kindness, lowliness, meekness and patience. We have to adopt a viewpoint that does not come naturally; it is God's attitude to us, that of the owner at the recovery of his lost property; it is not the way we usually think of one another.

One of the firmest and most central convictions of the Christians from the beginning of the movement (e.g. in the preaching of John the Baptist) was that it is possible to change your mind and see everything in an entirely different way. We need not share the (very natural) disgruntlement of the older brother; we can share God's joy over the good things that happen to other people.

THE BEAM IN MY EYE

7th after Pentecost
ASB p.668

T HE WAY we see ourselves is quite different from the way other people see us, or we see them. Self-awareness is hard to come by. Nor does knowing that this is so make much difference to us; we apply the principle to other people; they are the ones who see motes in other people's eyes and have beams in their own.

We do, however, have enough self-knowledge to identify with the millionaire debtor in today's gospel (Matthew 18.21-end). He has recently been shattered by the threat that he will be sold into slavery, with his wife and his children, and all his property will be forfeited. The fear of the king remains with him, even when he has been told that his debt has been cancelled; it takes more than mercy to dispel terror, and he is still in shock. He therefore imitates the king by demanding payment from a fellow servant, even though the sum involved is ridiculously small in comparison with his own debt. The inappropriateness of what he is doing does not strike him; instead of that, he feels he must re-establish his position through being harsh with other people. It was his rigorous pursuit of power that got him his promotion in the first place; there would be no point in changing to kindness and softness now.

Those who are looking on see it in a different way and are horrified; but he is not. He must secure his position in the only way he knows.

The king's expectation that the man would have shared with others the generosity that he had received was misplaced. The man is blind to what has been done to him; it is as if it had never happened.

It is, of course, a terrible story, and it must leave us very unhappy – particularly the conclusion: "And that is how my heavenly Father will deal with you unless you each forgive your brother from your heart." It holds out little hope for us; it is pessimistic, as so much in Matthew's gospel is pessimistic, e.g. many go along the broad road to destruction, few on the narrow road to life (7.13f).

The English word "to criticize" means to act as a judge. No amount of mercy from God stops us from criticizing other people: from not obeying the law, but being judge, being God (see James 4.11f). We have been forgiven, but it has not taken; we do not find it inappropriate that we should not forgive.

Why did the compilers of the ASB translate the Greek in the Lord's Prayer as: "Forgive us our sins as we forgive those who sin against us", when the original clearly means: "as we have forgiven those who sin against us"? Was it because they knew that we had not?

TRUST THE SPIRIT

8th after Pentecost
ASB p.673

THE theme for this Sunday is The Fruit of the Spirit, and it may be that it is an idea that will solve two problems that worry us from time to time, one a practical problem, and the other more theoretical.

The practical problem is: How can we achieve the proper balance in our lives between attitudes and activities that seem in themselves to be opposites: firmness and gentleness; love and justice; work and rest; subtlety and innocence; joy and sorrow. If we try to put them together, will the result not be like that of mixing hot water with cold: that we shall become luke warm?

The theoretical problem is to do with what we should think about the Holy Spirit. The New Testament writers sometimes speak of the Spirit in personal terms; and the later Christian writers say that there are three persons in the Godhead; but when the Old Testament writers used the expression, The Spirit of God, no one thought they were talking about another person, distinct from God. Why should we believe in the personality of the Spirit?

Can we see it like this: we can leave the problem of the balance of our lives, putting together what seems incompatible, to God the Holy Spirit. We do not have to achieve the balance; we do not control the mix. The Spirit of God can be relied on to get it right. The Spirit is not an impersonal power, but is God dealing with us in as personal a way as the Father and the Son.

The expression, The Fruit of the Spirit, means what the Spirit does, what he achieves in our lives. (In the Jerusalem Bible, used in the ASB for this Sunday's epistle, it is translated as, What the Spirit brings, Galatians 5.12.) The Spirit is the subject; the fruit is his work.

If we think of the Spirit as personal, not impersonal, the practical problem is solved. So Paul says, at the end of the reading: Since the Spirit is our life, let us be directed by the Spirit.

PROTECTED BY THE NAME

9th after Pentecost
ASB p.678

MODERN TRANSLATIONS of the New Testament are made from the old manuscripts, both those that are written in Greek (the original language of all the writers) and those which are ancient translations from Greek into Coptic, Syriac, Latin, Armenian and so on. Unfortunately all these manuscripts are different from one another: no scribe can copy anything for long without making a mistake. The translators have, therefore, to choose between different texts. This happens to affect the gospel for this Sunday (John 17.11b-19). The translation that was chosen for the ASB is the Jerusalem Bible, which has:

'Holy Father, keep those you have given me true to your name . . .

'While I was with them, I kept those you had given me true to your name.'

The majority of editors and commentators, however, think that the original Greek was what is translated in the Revised English Bible, as follows:

'Holy Father, protect them by the power of your name, the name you have given me . . . While I was with them, I protected them by the power of your name which you gave me.'

A person's name was thought of as an extension of himself; to do things in somebody's name was to do them as if you were that person. The name is the person, whose name it is. God had given his name to Jesus, so that what Jesus did was what God does; he did the work of his Father. Now Jesus is asking that the name which God gave to him, that is, the power and authority to do God's will, will protect his disciples – it is for them that he is praying.

Jesus's prayer is that God will protect the disciples from evil, keep them together, and preserve them from destruction.

To belong to the followers of Jesus is not to belong to a merely human institution that carries on, as best it can, from one generation to the next. We are not moving further and further from Jesus, or from God, as the years go by. And it is not all up to us to keep the institution true to the ideals of the founder, as they apply to new situations in which we find ourselves.

The mistake is to think of the church as moving in a straight line from its beginning to its end, so that every day it is further from where it started. As the writer of the fourth gospel saw it, every generation is kept from evil by the name of God; every day we are as close to God as they were at the beginning of church history. Jesus prays for God to be to us as he was to him, and faith is trusting that this is how it really is. God is with us; his name protects us.

NEEDING HELP?

10th after Pentecost
ASB p.683

WHAT IS SO DIFFICULT about Christianity is that it makes us think of ourselves in a way that we have no wish to – it expects us to think that we need help; and that is the last thing we believe. We cannot be doing with the suggestion that we are not able to cope on our own. All the evidence is that in the majority of cases self-reliance becomes more important the older you are; and that that is how we like people to be. We prefer the old person who refuses to be helped to the one who no longer tries for herself. It is a mark against someone to say, She is becoming very dependent on her niece.

So we must identify ourselves with Peter in today's gospel (John 13.1–15) when he says, I will never let you wash my feet. No self-respecting person would let his host do this for him: just as we would not allow him to clean our shoes or brush our hair. If we had not heard the story before, we should have been horrified that Jesus had got round to Peter before anything was said. Had the other disciples no self-respect? If we saw our own children accepting an older person's help without demur, we should be furious with them; You lazy slob, we would say; get up and do it yourself; don't let your mother do it for you.

Our society teaches us self-reliance, but the gospel tells us that self-reliance is the barrier that makes faith in Christ impossible; if we rely on ourselves and think that we do not need the help that Jesus can give us, we isolate ourselves from him. If I do not wash you, he says, you are not in fellowship with me. The gospel and the world are still in conflict with one another.

Most of the day we must think about how we can get through it without being a burden to other people; but when it comes to reflection and prayer, we see that we have been carried all the way – by all sorts of people, and above all by Christ. We live off him. We must not let the self-reliance that we practise most of the day spill over into our relation with God, or into our gratitude for what other people do for us. In the end, it is our society that is wrong, and that has instilled into us a way of living that is impossible. A genuine humility would recognize that no one can be human without depending on other people. That is the way we are, and it is our blindness that prevents us from seeing it.

CHRISTIAN INCONGRUITY

11th after Pentecost
ASB p.688

WE SHALL NEVER make sense of the church, if we do not realize that it is an absurd institution. There is and there must be incongruity between what it says and what it is. Membership of the church puts you in an impossible position, in which you claim one thing but do the opposite; the only hope is if you know that this is what you are doing.

Take, for example, the words in today's gospel (John 13. 31–35): 'I give you a new commandment: love one another; just as I have loved you, you also must love one another. By this love you have for one another, everyone will know that you are my disciples.'

Somebody said the other day about poetry, People write best about being in love when they're not actually in love at all. This seems to fit the New Testament, too. The most anti-Jewish books in the New Testament are Matthew and John, and these are the books that say most about love.

We are absurd creatures: the people who paint the most beautiful pictures live the most sordid lives; the preachers who preach the most moving sermons are those who most need to hear them, and cannot.

The Jerusalem Bible translation of the gospel has exaggerated the absurdity of the situation. It does not say: By this love you have for one another, everyone will know that you are my disciples. No doubt they might, if we had it; but we know that we do not, and that the church never has: there have been rows among Christians from the beginning, and it continues so to the present day. If the original exclamation, How these Christians love one another! was meant seriously, it is not taken in that sense now, and it could not be.

73

In fact, what the gospel says is: If there is this love among you, then everyone will know that you are my disciples (REB). The promise is conditional, but the condition is unfulfilled.

We are on the way, we have not arrived; and it is essential to be aware of the difference. Anything here must be provisional, a botched job, and there must be incongruities. To attribute perfection to anything under the sun is to idolize it.

TODAY'S JOB

12th after Pentecost
ASB p.693

THE THEME for this Sunday is The Witnessing Community, and that means the community that points away from itself to – what? All sorts of answers suggest themselves: A better way of life; holiness; charity; forgiveness – we could go on for ever thinking of words that sum up, more or less adequately, the benefits of Christianity. This would be one way of pointing away from the church to what it is that it stands for, and the advantage of it would be that we should find new allies who would greet us as they also believed in a better way of life, holiness, charity, or forgiveness.

This week's epistle (2 Cor. 5. 14–6.2), however, sends us off in a different direction. Paul repeats the name 'Christ' again and again; elsewhere he uses it as an alternative to 'Jesus', without any obvious difference of meaning. If we had asked Paul what the community must point to, he would have said, To Jesus Christ: a man who had a day of birth and a day of death, and also a day of resurrection. We are not concerned with general ideas that can be expressed by abstract nouns (e.g. charity); we are concerned with a particular person who had, and has, a personal name; there was a time before he was born, and our community looks back to him as its beginning. He changed the situation through what he did; now, there is a new world; the old order has gone, and a new order has already begun.

The great advantage of thinking in this way, instead of thinking in general terms (morality, holiness etc.) is that it leaves far more room for manoeuvre. There is very little abstract thinking in the New Testament; there is much more of telling stories, and the stories are about people. People are richer, as sources of inspiration, than ideas; we respond to individuals far more than to policies, though politicians wish it were not so, and we can understand why.

Moreover, what the witnessing community believes is that the person to whom it points is not a past figure, but one who is present and contemporary; and this creates even more room for manoeuvre. There is much in the past of the church that we must dissociate ourselves from: there will always be new work to be undertaken which had never been on the church's agenda before. We are like the workmen on a building-site, receiving our instructions from the foreman for the things to be done, today.

THE UNPOPULARITY OF PROPHETS

13th after Pentecost
ASB p. 698

A NYONE reading the description of the death of Stephen (Acts 7.54–8.1. today's New Testament reading) will be reminded of the last words of Jesus before his death, as they are described in Luke's gospel: Jesus said, Father, forgive them (23.34) and Stephen says, Lord, do not hold this sin against them; Jesus said, Father, into your hands I commit my spirit (23.46) and Stephen says, Lord Jesus receive my spirit. The disciple follows the pattern of his master. Luke had recorded in his gospel a saying of Jesus that had promised that this was how it would be: Everyone who is fully trained shall be as his teacher (6.40).

It has been recognized for a long time that this idea contributed to the way in which Luke composed his second volume, the Acts of the Apostles. At the end of Acts, there is a close parallel between what happens to Paul and what had happened to Jesus: both go to Jerusalem, are arrested and tried before Jews and Romans: Jesus dies and rises, Paul is shipwrecked and saved; Jesus preaches to the disciples in Jerusalem, Paul to the Jews in Rome. (This may explain the surprising ending of Acts: the pattern has been completed, so we do not need to know what happened to Paul next.)

The Spirit which came upon Mary and made it possible for her to conceive Jesus comes upon the church at Pentecost in order that the disciples may be as their teacher. They will not be over and above their teacher (Luke 6.40), in the sense that they will not be more popular than Jesus: Stephen is put to death, and Paul is still a prisoner when Acts comes to an end. The Jews in Rome say that all they know about the sect is that no one has a good word to say for it (Acts 28.22). To be like Jesus does not mean to be accpetable to those who are in authority, either in the state or in the church. Luke had made this clear in the sermon on the plain:

Alas for you when all speak well of you:
that is how their fathers treated the false prophets (6.26).

It would be a mistake to think that because the church is ridiculed and despised, it is therefore doing what it should be doing; but it would not be a mistake to think that if the church is doing what it should be doing, it will be ridiculed and despised. There can be good reasons and bad reasons for being unpopular, but unpopularity is what the Spirit will produce in the followers of Jesus.

LOVE IT AND HATE IT

14th after Pentecost
ASB p. 703

A VERSE from the early chapters of Genesis is quoted in two of this Sunday's readings: That is why a man leaves his father and mother and attaches himself to his wife, and the two become one (2.24). The passage appealed to the author of the Letter to the Ephesians because he saw how it could be applied to the new situation in which he and his readers found themselves: one who believed in Christ must 'leave' his natural family to join the church which is the bride of Christ, while still fulfilling the duties required by family commitments (Ephesians 5.25–6.4).

Mark places the paragraph in which Jesus quotes the same verse from Genesis (10.2–16) in the section describing the journey to Jerusalem and the teaching about discipleship. To follow Jesus involves leaving father (1.20), home, brothers, sisters, mother, children, land (10.29); in fact, as Peter says, Everything (10.28). Mark also shows that this was how it was for Jesus: his family said: He is out of his mind. Jesus said, of those who were sitting

77

in a circle about him: Here are my mother and my brothers – not those who were outside (3.21, 31–35).

New Testament writers recognize that the family is an ambiguous institution, that can be both a blessing and a curse. It can give us security, and it can restrain us from entering into the freedom of faith. It can help us to grow up, and it can stop us from being mature. It can make slaves of us, but it can also release us into being ourselves. We must love it, but we must also hate it (Luke 14.26).

It must be because the family is such a powerful institution, capable of affecting people so deeply, that it has this ambiguous quality. The Old Testament reading for this Sunday is the description of the good wife (Proverbs 31.10-end), And as you read it, you think of women you have known fulfil the description. They are not the sort of people one would lightly disagree with, and it would not be difficult to understand how their sons had to leave their father and mother in order to be attached to their wives.

What is true of the family is true of any other institution that has a powerful influence upon us; it can be a destructive force, acting in opposition to God's Spirit and his love.

OBLIGATIONS

15th after Pentecost
ASB p.708

T HE SORT OF PERSON who really gets us down is the one who takes everything for granted, and seems to have no idea of gratitude or indebtedness. They use your telephone without offering to pay for the call; they take everything you set before them and never say, Thank you. We cannot be doing with them; have they no sense of obligation?

The conflict between Jesus and the Pharisees and Herodians in today's gospel (Matthew 22.15–22) revolves round the contrast between what is permissible and what is obligatory. The question is asked in the form: Is it permissible to give (not, as in JB translation, pay) taxes to Caesar or not? The answer is, Give back (or, pay) to Caesar what belongs to Caesar – and to God what belongs to God. The way to understand the situation is not to think in terms of options that I am free to choose between, but of an obligation that is laid upon me. If I do not see myself in this way, I have missed the truth.

The head and name on the coin remind us of our duty to the state; that duty leaves us no choice as to whether we pay taxes or whether we do not. Anybody who thinks they have an option has not seen what the situation really is; they have a mental block.

And the defect that prevents them from acknowledging their debt to the state may also prevent them from being aware of their duty to God. The same blindness to obligations can happen in both spheres. So Jesus adds: And to God what belongs to God.

What belongs to Caesar is limited: so much tax. There is no limit to what belongs to God, because he is the maker and giver of everything there is. For each person, what belongs to God is the whole of that person's existence; and the obligation is to pay God back with yourself. Earlier in the gospel, Jesus had told his disciples that he had to go to Jerusalem and be put to death, and Peter had rebuked him: No, Lord, this shall never happen to you. Jesus had to give himself back to God, and his followers have to do the same.

The Pharisees and the Herodians went away, having lost the point. Their flattery of Jesus recoiled on them and they were shown up as people without a sense of obligation, the sort of people we cannot be doing with. Beware: the answer of Jesus to them is more comprehensive than we thought. Our obligation is to give ourselves, and that is more than we expected or intended.

WHY IS THE SAMARITAN GOOD?

16th after Pentecost
ASB p.713

T HE STORY of the Samaritan, which is this week's gospel (Luke 10.25–37) contrasts two people who did nothing to help the man in distress, with one person who acted with extreme generosity; we are told to imitate him, not them. Why?

To answer that question, we need to notice that the story tells us something further about the two people who did nothing, and about the one person who acted generously: they were temple-officials (a priest and a Levite); he was not an Israelite, but a Samaritan. That is to say, the characters who are not to be imitated are representatives of one aspect of religion that is expressed in corporate worship; whereas the character in the story who is to be taken as our example is an outsider, in every sense.

It would be possible to think of a religion that was completely expressed in performances that took place in a designated building and according to fixed regulations, and neither needed nor sought further expression in life outside – like the musical banks in Samuel Butler's *Erewhon*. And it would be possible to think of a religion that dispensed with buildings, performances and rites, and was expressed entirely in a particular style of living. What we must say about the story of the Samaritan is that it seems to point us in the direction of the second of these two ideas of a religion, rather than in that of the first. Why?

The answer may lie in the Old Testament reading (Leviticus 19.9–18) with its repeated statement, I am the Lord. The question about religion has to be a question about God. Is he the centre of a system that involves rites and ceremonies; or is he the loving heart at the core of the universe?

Of course it can be said that it is artificial and unnecessary to pose the question in the form of these opposites; but in reply to that it must be pointed out that it is not we who started this, but the story of the priest, the Levite and the Samaritan, and whoever it was who first told it; and that we can hardly listen to the story without thinking about the contrasted characters and what they stand for.

Greek-speaking Christians of the first century seem to have taken over a word that had usually meant 'property', or 'goods', and applied it to mean 'goodness', 'generosity', doing the sort of thing the Samaritan did. Perhaps they felt there was a gap in their vocabulary; nothing to say when you wanted to talk about kindness, loving care, putting yourself out for other people.

When we read the New Testament, and when we read the Old (which is where it all started), we are aware of people who believed that they were closer to doing God's will when they were being actively good, than at any other time; and who thought that this was so, because God himself was all goodness.

WHAT COUNTS IS DOING

17th after Pentecost
ASB p.717

THERE IS A MAN in Mark's gospel who asks the question, What must I do to gain possession of eternal life? and he is told what to do: he is to keep the commandments (Mark 10. 17–22). When another man asks virtually the same question in Acts, What must I do to be saved? he is told to believe (Acts 16.30f). The difference between faith and action is not just a matter of words; it has exercised the minds of our predecessors, from the earliest days of Christianity, and it is part of the Jewishness of Christianity. (See, for example, this Sunday's Old Testament reading, Jeremiah 7. 1–11: faith in the temple is no excuse for living an immoral life.)

You could say that the closer Christians kept to Judaism, the greater the emphasis on action. Matthew's gospel is an example: it is no good saying Lord, Lord, or prophesying, or exorcising, or performing many miracles; what counts is doing the Father's will, and that has been defined in the earlier chapters of the sermon (Matthew 7.21ff). Similarly, in the final speech (chapters 23–25), there are no questions about believing; everything is determined by what you have done or not done. The Son of Man will reward everyone according to performance (*praxis*, 16.27).

Another example of the Jewishness of Christianity asserting itself against an excessive emphasis on faith is the Letter of James. The writer knows people who say they have faith, but their actions do nothing to show it. Faith, he says, if it does not lead to action, is by itself a useless thing (James 2.14ff.)

And in today's gospel (Luke 17. 11–19) the one who is praised by Jesus is the one who came back and thanked him; Jesus says to him, Your faith has saved you; and this faith was shown in the action of returning and thanking.

It may, possibly, be right for us to thank God that we are English people, not French or German or anything else; we are not noted for being intellectuals, but to us what appeals most is what is practical. If a difference in doctrine would make no conceivable difference to what you do, why bother about it, we think. Ideas, as such, do not attract us; we readily consent to the proposition that actions speak louder than words, and that it is what you do that matters, not what you say. In spite of all the disadvantages of being English (hypocrisy, smugness, classconsciousness, traditionalism, etc.) there is one thing for which we can be grateful: we are not likely to think theology matters more than morality, or what you believe than what you do.

A GENEROUS SPIRIT

18th after Pentecost
ASB p.722

OF ALL THE THINGS we want and need, the most important and necessary is this: a generous spirit. We want to love, without any limit and without any impurity. Above all, we want to love you; that is what you have told us to do, and we do want to do it.

We know that we do not love you as we should. We work on the principle, How little can I get away with? What is the minimum I must give you? We know, with our heads, that you are not mocked; but in practice we live as though you did not know the secrets of our hearts. We seem to have to deceive ourselves, and lie to ourselves, in order to cope with you at all.

What we want and need is a generosity of spirit that is pure — willing one thing, single-minded. This is what we never do. We always have a double motive, and aim at two birds with every throw: to be seen to do what is right; to be praised for doing it; to be admired for our performance. We spoil everything by not putting the whole of our will into doing it with the straightforward intention of glorifying your holy name. We do not, and we cannot, please you, without you.

If we had what we lack, we would be able to put up with far more than we can stand as things are with us now. We are far too dependent on approval, praise, thanks, and on a sense of achievement, success, feeling good in ourselves. We should ask for only sufficient success, and the amount that is sufficient should be diminishing towards zero, far faster than it is. If we are to love you unconditionally and without limit, there should be no need of any reassurance.

Fortunately for us, we still find one kind of character very attractive. We still feel the pull of those who make no compromises, but are whole-hearted, whole-hoggers – whatever it is they do. We say, I admire this devotion to duty; and we know it should be so with us, and we long for it to be so. Give us, therefore, a generous spirit, to love you.

That is your first commandment, and if we could do that, then we might be able to do the second also, and love our neighbour as someone like ourselves. Jesus put them in this order: God; neighbour. If our love for you were unsullied by love of other things, it might spill over with love for our neighbours.

Give us what we most need and do not have: a generous spirit.

JESUS ANNOYS US

19th after Pentecost
ASB p.728

W HAT do we go to church for? Out of a sense of duty;
because we are members of a body; to receive grace; as
an act of witness; to encourage one another and to be encouraged
by others; to give and to receive – we could go on thinking of
reasons for going to church for a long time, but we might not
hit upon one reason that fits the readings for this Sunday
particularly, and may be important every week. We go to
church to be annoyed, embarrassed, made to squirm, pricked in
the conscience, shaken, stirred, insulted.

The sayings of Jesus in Matthew (e.g. 6.24-end, this Sunday's
gospel) will do this for us: No anxious thoughts about food and
drink and clothes; no anxiety about the future; tomorrow will
look after itself. It is not the way we live now, and there is no
point in pretending that it is. The one who speaks to us in the
gospels is a total foreigner to us and our world. All he can do is
annoy us and make us squirm. The important thing is to see that
this is how it is meant to be. We go to church for this, among
many other reasons: we go to church to be made to feel uncomfortable.

We know that we need to be treated in this way, and that there
are far too few people who will do it to us. Most of the people we
meet in the week go out of their way to be pleasant, and to leave
us feeling happier than we were before. We know, however, that
complacency is a deadly evil that grows over us like some weed
that kills everything in its way. We have got to be shaken out of
it. The sayings of Jesus in the gospels do this; and the preacher is
there to make us uncomfortable. His job is to stir us up.

He has to overcome our inertia, and that will mean that he must
apply pressure to us that is exceptional and more than we can

resist. Objects that are stationary require more force to get them into motion than objects that are already moving. The preacher faces a more-or-less inert congregation; and the congregation faces the preacher with some well-grounded suspicion, knowing it does not want to be moved. We must pray for the preacher, that he will do to us what we do not want him to do. We must attend to this foreigner, who enters the twentieth century from the first, and talks what sounds to us like nonsense; or if it is not nonsense, it is an insult to our way of life.

If Jesus and his agent the preacher can make you cross, thank God for it. Something has happened – something that was meant to happen, had to happen.

IS THERE ANY HOPE?

20th after Pentecost
ASB p.733

IF we could bring Paul to visit our churches, and then discuss with him the differences between us and the congregations he had founded in the first century, at some point in the conversation he would surely have said: I do not find much evidence that you are longing for the future. You seem to me to have settled in to the present and to have accepted it; even, in some cases, to prefer the past, and to have half an eye on that. What has happened to hope? With us, it was one third of the three-fold cord: Faith, Love and Hope.

Paul puts his finger on an obvious difference between then and now. We are suspicious of dissatisfaction; we think it wrong to complain about life as it is, and a fault to be forever wanting something better. We have accepted the idea that we should make do with what we have, be thankful and content.

86

Paul and his first-century believers, perhaps because many of them had been brought up as Jews, had no such attitude. They thought that the best was just about to come, in the future; therefore the present was a time of waiting and of putting up with troubles while longing for them to cease. We groan, he says; we wait, we hope, we endure.

The advantage of Paul's point of view over ours is that his takes far more account of the way things actually are in the world. If we have to be content with life as it is, we shall have to shut out from our consciousness everything that is unjust, deplorable, disastrous. We shall have to be highly selective. Hope, on the other hand, feeds on discontent; and discontent, in turn, feeds on awareness of evil.

Moreover, it is not as though there were any shortage of ills, or as though we were ignorant of them. It may (it must) have been different for people of some classes in society in the eighteenth and nineteenth centuries; they could have been ignorant of a great deal that was happening elsewhere: we cannot; the information is delivered to our houses daily.

What is called for is the belief that we live in a temporary, interim state; that life as it is now is deplorable and that it is only possible to believe in a good God, who has sole responsibility for the world, if there is to be a better future. Faith has to breed hope, or it will strangle itself.

FAMILIARITY KILLS

21st after Pentecost
ASB p.738

A STRONG case can be made for the idea that our worst and most insidious enemy is one that is never even mentioned in scripture: familiarity. Neither the word itself, nor any synonym, ever occurs. Perhaps the nearest that the Biblical writers get to referring to it is when they make use of the theme of blindness; because, if familiarity is the cause of contempt, it is familiarity that is blinding our eyes and making us incapable of seeing what is going on around us.

The widow who wants justice, on the other hand, will not stop knocking on the judge's door to demand action; her situation is such that she will not, cannot, let the matter rest. No amount of familiarity with her plight will stop her from being tiresome. The followers of Jesus, similarly, should be at God, day and night, calling upon him to begin to rule over the world, and to abolish the injustice that is rampant. But will they succumb to familiarity with the way things are, and cease to cry out? Will there be no faith on the earth, because believers will have stopped seeing and feeling the iniquity of the world as it is? (Luke 18.1ff).

The widow will go on with her demands, until she receives her rights. The danger with the disciples is that they will settle for less and accept some substitute for the new world in which there will be no more crying. They may stop complaining and resign themselves to the familiarity of evil (saying, This is how things have always been, and always will be), because they have been brought off by their own good luck and prosperity; hence the warnings earlier in this gospel:

Alas for you who are rich.
Alas for you who are well-fed now.

Alas for you who laugh now.
Alas for you when all speak well of you (6.24ff).

The best way to beat familiarity is by prayer. Prayer takes hold of the injustice in the world, and demands that God intervene. Prayer will not let the matter drop, or allow us to become used to the situation; prayer requires us to feel the plight of those who are in misery.

Just as we need artists and poets to make us see what is before us all the time, though we have stopped noticing it: so we need prophets to keep on opening our eyes to what is going on, and to make us pray; then we shall experience the contradiction between the way things are, and the will of God. This is faith. The question Jesus asks is, Will it continue?

BE MORE CUNNING

22nd after Pentecost
ASB p.742

WE are being rebuked in today's gospel (the dishonest steward, Luke 16. 1–9) and what we are being rebuked for is our lack of shrewdness. We should be more cunning, we are told, more like the agent who reduced his master's bills so that he might have somewhere to live when he was sacked.

It is surprising to find this in one of the gospels; but in fact it is not confined to Luke; Matthew has it, too: Jesus tells his disciples to be as cunning as serpents, referring back to the well-known passage in Genesis: The serpent was the most cunning of all the creatures the Lord God had made (Matthew 10.16, Genesis 3.1).

What are we to be cunning about? Here, again, the answer is

surprising. We are to secure our own future by the way we use our money now. We are to buy our way into salvation.

One thing is clear: simple and clear-cut distinctions between what is right and what is wrong can be misleading. Christians are not to forsake intelligence, wisdom, using their sense. They are not to be simplistic monomaniacs with bees in their bonnets and King Charles' head.

For example, we are not to think that everything will be done for us, and that our co-operation is not needed; that we are saved apart from our works. The collect reminds us that our wills are involved, and that they must be stirred up. We are expected to do good works. We are to look forward to rewards. We are to work for our future.

One of the occupational hazards of the religious life is that we become obsessed with fewer and fewer ideas; rejecting more and more, as we concentrate on less and less. It is a prescription for being a bore. The gospel rebukes us for this, and requires us to entertain a greater variety of ideas. The reality is a very rich mix.

TOO GOOD TO BE TRUE?

Last Sunday after Pentecost
ASB p.745

GOD'S PROMISES, we say in this Sunday's collect, exceed all that we can desire. It is a good thing that they do; they would not be worth thinking about, if they were equal to them. He promises new heavens and a new earth, as the introductory sentence (2 Peter 3.13) reminds us; we would have been satisfied with a few minor adjustments to the present heavens and the present earth, but what is promised is a complete overhaul, a universe in which righteousness will dwell. We shall have new and transfigured bodies, Paul says (Philippians 3.7-end), to live in a world that is wholly obedient to the will of God in every part.

It will be what we have prayed for every day: God will be adored by all his creatures; he will rule over everything, and what will happen will be his will and nothing else. We have said it again and again; it will happen, and it will be better than we ever thought.

Excess is the hallmark of God: too much food in the feeding miracles; too many people being healed for anyone to have a rest; too much forgiveness for the Pharisees to cope with; too many crowds for anyone to get in at the door. The activity of Jesus is excessive, as you would expect, if he comes from God. And his message is excessive too: he jumps the gun, and has meals with the sinners.

The best way to dismiss it is to say it is too good to be true. But why should God's ways be determined by us? And if we fix the limits, how shall we recognize him if he exceeds them? And he does: everything he does is marked by (what we think of as) overdoing it.

It is not only his gifts; it is also what he requires of us. He will not be satisfied with a bit: he insists on having us whole. His demands exceed our ability to give. But it does not matter, because his grace is always more than we needed.

Who would have thought of his giving us the life of Christ, and the Holy Spirit to work in us? Who would have thought that we could be renovated and transfigured into being partners of God? His goodness baffles our meanness and his excess silences our sobriety and moderation.

ASB YEAR TWO

PRAISE THE MAKER OF EVERYTHING

9th before Christmas
ASB p.398

T HE twenty-four elders say that God is worthy to be praised, because he created everything; there was nothing, they assert, that came into existence except by his will. It needs a greater insight and knowledge than we have, into our world and the reason why it is as we know it to be, to be able to say such a thing. Whether we look inwards or outwards, there is too much to deplore for us to be able to say to God, Thank you for making everything just as it is.

This is so, not because things are worse now than they were at the time when John wrote The Revelation; he lived in bad times and he expected even worse to follow soon. He foresaw the final collapse of the Roman Empire, which he dubbed Babylon; he believed it to be thoroughly evil, and he had no illusions about its power and majesty. How could he be so positive, then, in his description of the elders' praise of God the Creator? How could they be so approving?

The vision of the throne and the One who sat upon it comes early in his book; there is much to follow. There is, for example, the Lamb slain for people of every tribe and language, nation and race, which comes next, and is closely associated with the throne and the elders. He is the symbol of redemption. Then there is the whole narrative of tribulation and woe, which turn out in the end to have been purifying and recreative. John refers to this by what is, in this sort of literature, a technical expression: What must happen hereafter; it means God's unfinished business with the world.

The twenty-four elders, we must assume, know all that has to be done; they can see the whole process of creation and redemption as one act of God, in a way that we cannot. They know that God will not fail, but that what he does will be an unqualified success.

Everything will all come together in a renewed heaven and earth, and in a city in which God and his creatures will share eternal joy and blessedness.

It is only right and possible to thank God for making the world and us, because there is more to be said, more to be believed, and more to be done. It would be a mistake, according to John's vision, to think that the existence of evil made praise and thanksgiving for creation impossible. In spite of how things are now, and how they will be in the immediate future, he who was, and is, and is to come, is enthroned, and will complete what he has begun.

A CURE FOR SELF-DECEPTION

8th before Christmas
ASB p.403

WHAT calls out to be affirmed this Sunday is the desperateness of our situation and what follows from this: the nature of the cure that we need. The point that has to be made, as clearly and firmly as possible, is that telling us what to do is no remedy for our plight. No law or commandment or advice will deliver us; and we know why this is so, through putting together the old story in Genesis 3 and Paul's commentary on it in Romans 7.

If being told what to do (and what not to do) had ever been enough, then surely Adam and Eve would never have eaten the forbidden fruit in Paradise: they knew, and knew from God, exactly what they must and must not do. But we have freedom to twist things, and to twist them, as we think, to our advantage. The command not to eat the fruit of one tree suddenly appears to be designed to prevent us from receiving benefits that would be to our greatest advantage; God, we think, is deliberately excluding us from good things that he does not want us to have; we attribute meanness and malice to him. He is against us, we suppose: so we follow our own inclinations which point us to our advantage, rather than the divine law which seems to exclude us and hinder us.

We have the capacity to deceive ourselves, and to attribute hostility and meanness to our creator. People as perverse as this can turn anything into anything: good into evil, and gifts into restrictions. This is why telling us what to do will never cure our problem; we shall always think of an excellent reason to resist, and persuade ourselves that we are right to do so.

What kind of help do we need? Only a gift that can overcome all our opposition and perversity. We shall have to be brought into association with the truth, and this will be painful; but knowing ourselves as we do, we shall accept that what is needed is what we have not got; that it must take the place of our twisted selves, and act in us. The truth must overcome the lie, and the light must banish the darkness in us.

In another old story, the Israelites were healed through looking at a serpent of brass on a pole; what is offered now is light that draws us to itself, so that it enables us to see that God is in all that we do (John 3.21, REB).

GOD BELIEVES IN US

7th before Christmas
ASB p.407

G OD acts first; explanations are arrived at later. The first Christians found themselves searching for ways of understanding what had happened: Why had Jesus died, and why had God raised him from the dead? They said it was according to the scriptures and they meant by that that there had been promises and predictions in the law and the prophets and the psalms. They read the texts in order to make sense of what had happened.

One of the passages that helped most was the story of Abraham and the sacrifice of Isaac; and one way to take it was to say that Jesus was God's only Son, and that his death was the sacrifice that dealt with the sin of the world.

The identification of Jesus as the one and only, beloved, dear Son of the Father comes in the first three gospels; it is there in the words of the voice from heaven at the Baptism and at the Transfiguration; it is also there in the parable of the vineyard. Moreover it lies behind a passage in Paul's Letter to the Romans: God, like Abraham, did not spare his own Son (8.32).

Abraham had acted in faith: it was because of his faith that he had obeyed the terrible command to sacrifice Isaac. Abraham believed God; but when God did not spare his own Son, whom did he believe?

The answer must be, God believed in us. He believed that the death of Jesus would effect our salvation. We can see that this was how Paul thought from what he says next in the Letter to the Romans: He did not spare his own Son, but gave him up for us all; how can he fail to lavish every other gift upon us? The death of Jesus is understood as the sign of God's good will towards us; God is on our side; he believes in us.

We tell people we believe in them, when their future is at stake; when they are the subject of rumour and scandal; when they are undergoing a test or sitting an examination. In times of anxiety what we need above all is someone who says they believe in us.

No doubt it is important to believe in God; but it is far more important that he believes in us. The continuance of our faith is uncertain; we cannot be sure what we shall do; we may pack it all in and become agnostic. Fortunately there is more to be said than that. Our maker has confidence in us. He has not made us in vain, and his purpose will not be thwarted. Our faithlessness will not cancel the faithfulness of God (Romans 3.3.)

If we can see that our faith in God is the result of God's faith in us, we shall be less likely to worry about losing it. We are sustained in faith by the almighty believer; so there is nothing to fear – not even that we might fall from him.

FROM SLAVERY TO FREEDOM

6th before Christmas
ASB p.413

WHEN we think of Moses, we think of the law: What did Moses command you? Jesus asks. But before he is presented as the one who brings the law of God to the Israelites, we are told something else about him: that God will use him to bring them from Egypt to the promised land. Moses is told by

God to say to the Israelites: I will release you . . . I will rescue you . . . I will redeem you . . . I will adopt you . . . I will become your God . . . I will lead you . . . I will give you the land (Exodus 3.7ff).

The narrative that follows in the rest of the Pentateuch and Joshua and Judges shows how this happened: they left Egypt; they journeyed through the wilderness; they arrived at the promised land and eventually settled there. But all the time, from even before they left Egypt, throughout the years in the wilderness, and after they had settled in the land, they were disobedient to God and rebellious; a typical instance is when they said: If only we had died at the Lord's hand in Egypt, where we sat by the fleshpots and had plenty of bread! (Exodus 16.3).

Moses and Jesus are alike: both are involved in bringing people from one situation to another; in both cases, the journey is from slavery to freedom; and in both cases those who are being taken from deprivation and poverty to riches and wealth complain that they are being ill-treated; they would rather go back than go forward.

Our Egypt and our starting point is the self-centredness in which we grew up. We knew nothing else except that everyone should do what we wanted, and what would please us. These were our flesh-pots. As we were led away from them, to hear that we should rather love God and our neighbour, and abandon selfishness, we yearned to be back in the comfort we had known.

God is leading his people from a life of restrictions and routines, to liberty: he had told Moses to tell the Israelites I will adopt you; I will become your God. He takes away anything that inhibits his freedom with us, and ours with him. He does not want us to be children, but adults; the freedom he is bringing us into requires us to be mature.

The Peter Pan in us complains, and wants to go back to the starting-point; like the Galatians, we reject maturity and choose instead to be under rules and regulations. The Israelites were a burden to Moses, as the church is to Christ. God's gift is greater then our capacity to receive; we cannot cope with the generosity of his purpose.

THE END OF EVERYTHING

5th before Christmas
ASB p.417

THE end of the year: everything comes to an end. The Scriptures are full of it: Destruction is decreed (Isaiah 10.22); The sun will be darkened, the moon will not give her light; and the stars will come falling from the sky, the celestial powers will be shaken (Mark 13.24f). We deal with a God who brings things to an end, and we do not want to accept it.

Yet we should be able to recognize it as an indisputable fact. Most of us know little more than the names of our ancestors two or three generations back; most of the people who have lived on the earth are now unknown, forgotten; and so shall we be. The places where we have lived will also disappear along with Nineveh and Carthage and the rest of the cities of the ancient world.

The author of Ecclesiastes faced it: Those who lived in the past are not remembered, and those who follow will not be remembered by those who follow them. Everything is futile. He looked at destruction without shrinking, and accepted it as a fact.

It would be a mistake to think that because Christians believe in the resurrection of the dead, a new heaven and a new earth, and the life of the world to come, they can therefore avoid the fact of the coming destruction of themselves and of the planet on which they live. We are to believe in death and resurrection; resurrection does not cancel out or take away the inevitability of death: it is the dead that will be raised. Every Christian man and woman from the first century to the late nineteenth century has died. The conditions that make life on this planet possible for human beings will not, we are told, last for ever. Everything, in our part of the universe at least, will come to an end.

How are we to relate to a God who destroys what he had made? The Lord gives, and the Lord takes away; blessed be the name of the Lord. It must be with thanks for all that has been – however hard it may be to believe it at certain times; it cannot be right to wish that nothing had ever existed, including ourselves. And it must be with thanks that everything will stop; it cannot be right to wish to go on for ever, just as we are now; or for this world as it is to have no end. We resent the existence of non-biodegradable rubbish in the ditches and hedges along the footpaths, and long for the time when all wrappers, tins, cartons and containers will be made of fast-disappearing substances; thank goodness we live in bodies that have destruction built into them, and in a world that will come to an end. Permanence for ourselves, in our repeated resistance to grace, and for the world in its internal conflicts, would be intolerable.

Isaiah says, Destruction is decreed, overflowing with righteousness. It is good that creation is temporary and that time will stop. Whatever we believe about the world to come, we must be glad that this world will not go on for ever. The righteous God will not allow it to, because he is righteous. Blessed be the name of the Lord.

THE PRESENCE OF THE SUFFERING CHRIST

Advent Sunday
ASB p.422

ONE of the differences between Matthew's gospel and Mark's is that in Mark the emphasis is on the future coming of Jesus at the end of the world (What I say to you, I say to everyone: Keep awake. He is going ahead of you into Galilee: there you will see him, as he told you), whereas in Matthew the emphasis is on the presence of Christ with his disciples from the resurrection on. (Emmanuel, God is with us. Where two or three meet together in my name, I am there among them. I will be with you always, to the end of time.)

The last line of the book, the assurance of Christ's presence, shows the reader how the book is to be read: almost any paragraph in it can be used to answer the question, When we meet in Christ's name, and he is present, what is he here to do? Sometimes the answer is, He is here to proclaim to us the coming of the kingdom of Heaven, and to remind us of the judgement to come. Sometimes it is to teach us what we must do and be in order to enter the kingdom. And sometimes it is to offer us the healing and forgiveness that we shall need if we are to follow him through temptation and destruction.

But it would be a mistake to think that this is all that Matthew has to say about the meaning of Christ's presence with his church. Taken alone, it might suggest a Christ of power and majesty.

Matthew wants us also to see that the present Christ is the suffering Christ; and, to draw his readers attention to this, he puts the allegory of the sheep and the goats at the conclusion of the final speech of Jesus (25.31ff).

103

The judge who is also the king has continued to be hungry and thirsty, a stranger and naked, ill and in prison, because of his complete union with his brothers and sisters, the members of the church. He is in need, because they are in need; and they are in need, because they have followed his teaching and become the poor and the persecuted.

As Matthew sees it, the church is nearer to Christ when it has to receive help, than when it gives help; it is more blessed to receive than to give, he would have said. And there is no difficulty about seeing that this must be so: all that we hate about ourselves (pride, self-concern, self-righteousness and so on) is fed and expressed in doing good to others; all that we hope to avoid (humiliation, dependence, broken-heartedness) is built up by allowing others to do good to us – and to Christ.

In the next two verses, Jesus foretells for the last time his coming crucifixion; before that, in the allegory, he is bringing his followers down to his own level of shame and disgrace. It is a difficult message for a consumer society to hear and receive.

GOOD NEWS FOR THE POOR

2nd in Advent
ASB p.426

L UKE opens his account of the ministry of Jesus with the sermon in the synagogue at Nazareth; it is the first of many sermons that Luke will record, the last of them being Paul's final word in Acts 28; and it may be that Luke regarded it as in some ways the model for what all sermons should be. There is exposition of scripture (Isaiah 61.1,2) and application of it to the congregation (Today in your very hearing this text has come true).

The text and the exposition of it inform us of what it is to be a member of the congregation: it is to receive good news if one is poor enough to hear it; to be released from prison; to see instead of being blind, and to be free instead of broken; it is to know that the time of God's favour is now.

What offends the hearers at Nazareth is the generosity of God towards them and, as Jesus will go on to say, towards those who are outside Israel; as in the past, God's mercy will overflow all limits. It is his undeserved kindness that is too much for us, putting to shame the way in which we draw lines and refuse to go beyond them.

The congregation at Nazareth wanted to kill the preacher by throwing him over the edge of a hill; the only way in which we can avoid repeating their reaction to the good news will be by concentrating on that part of the text from Isaiah that explains who it is that will receive what is said: the poor, the prisoners, the blind, the broken victims. The passage from Isaiah will only come true today, if we see these words as the description of ourselves: the poverty of our response to God; the habits and assumptions that hold us captive; our inability to see more than a fraction of the truth about us; our need of restoration to wholeness.

The good news requires its hearers to adopt an attitude to themselves that is the opposite of the way that they prefer to think. If it cannot rouse them to awareness of need, it will not be good news for them, but only something that makes them angry; they will be in the deplorable state of people to whom no news is good news.

PREPARING FOR CHRIST

3rd in Advent
ASB p.432

JOHN the Baptist stands before us, on this Sunday, blocking the way to Christmas. We might think, Do we need a messenger sent ahead, when the Lord has already arrived? Can we not forget John the Baptist, now that Jesus has come? Who needs a herald, once the king is here?

But there is an order that must be followed, a sequence of ideas that must be observed, or we shall not come to the goal. The rule is: Repentance before faith; awareness of sickness before acceptance of cure; readiness for information before the information can profitably be given with any expectation that it will be received.

Anyone who teaches, knows that this is how it is. And parents know it too. There are matters that it is no use raising with others, because they are not yet ready to receive them; if you break the rule and hold forth, their eyes glaze over, they lose interest and get bored.

In order to be ready for Christ we must go back to John the Baptist and his message: Repent, there is one coming who is mightier than I. We shall have to get into the messy and unsatisfactory business of self-awareness, regret, sorrow for what we have done and not done, and longing to change and be changed, before we shall be able to listen to John's announcement of Jesus and his words of forgiveness. Readiness for Jesus requires us to pass through the school of John.

But there is more to it than this. Jesus is only known to us through his agents; there is no direct access or open vision. His agents are known to us more clearly than he is. It is not entirely accidental that we know what John the Baptist wore and ate, but we do not know as much about the clothes and diet of Jesus. In Mark's gospel, the young man who wore a white robe was seen, not the risen Lord. It might also be true to say that we can form a clearer picture of each of the four evangelists, than of Jesus himself, who is, in a sense, always out of focus.

John the Baptist, like all the other agents of God through whom we believe, points us to Christ and tells us about him. We cannot dispense with them, until we see him face to face. They tell us what they see, and we have to go on listening to them; for the present, he stands in the shadow.

GOD HAS MOVED IN

4th in Advent
ASB p.436

THE message of this Sunday is the presence of God with his people. It is one way in which Jews and Christians think and talk about their faith; and the advantage of it over many other ways of imagining it, is that it is simpler, plainer, and can be understood by everybody. We all know the difference between present and absent, here and not here.

We also know, from an early age, the importance of neighbourhood. We can understand how it is that some people do not want certain kinds of people to move into their district, and the vehemence with which they will say, Not in my back yard. Neighbourhood, we know, is important: it can be affected for good or ill; we are glad when some people move in, and sad when others do so.

There had been hostility between us and God, and distance;

perhaps it had to be so, in order that we might come to him freely, not willy-nilly. Christmas is the celebration of the end of this hostility; God has come to live in our neighbourhood – that is the meaning of the birth of Jesus. And, as Matthew understands it, this being with us was not ended by the Ascension; the gospel concludes with the important explanation, I will be with you always, to the end of time – bringing us back to the first quotation from scripture at the beginning, Emmanuel, which means God with us.

God has come to live in our neighbourhood. So the value of our property has shot up; the way in which we think about our place and about ourselves has changed; glory rubs off on those who are associated with it, just as those who live in, or have ever had any connection, however slight, with the place that wins the cup, experience some of the exaltation of the team and their supporters.

God with us is a rich and many-sided idea, including within it the belief that he is our protector, helper, support; that he is for us and not against us, available and accessible. Some one has moved in, who will make all the difference to where we live: it will change the place only for good, and to a degree we cannot imagine.

WHAT YOU SEE AND WHAT YOU GET

Christmas day
ASB p.443

W E are meant to be reassured when we are told that what we see is what we get; the shop-keeper will not take inferior fruit from another box behind the stall; everything is open and above-board. But Christmas is not like that. The shepherds, in Luke's story, are told that what they will see is a baby, wrapped in swaddling clothes and lying in a manger; what he is, is a Saviour, Christ the Lord.

Luke combines bare fact with later reflection on it. The bare fact is that a woman gave birth to a baby who was subsequently called Jesus, a common name in that place and at that time. Only afterwards was its significance realized: it meant Saviour. (See the REB note on Matthew 1.21.)

It would be years before Jesus was thought of in this way. The earliest evidence was probably his ability to deal with mentally disturbed people, and with cripples and others who suffered from various illnesses. He also assured those who were got down by a sense of guilt, that God had forgiven them. Most of all, he delivered his closest followers, who had deserted him when he was arrested, from despair at their own failure to stand by him. They said, He died for us.

It is typical of God to begin with unexplained facts, and allow the interpretation of them to develop later. This is how it happened, historically, and this is how it happens to us, personally. We start off with very rudimentary ideas as to what Christianity is about and who Jesus is; and it is only with time and experience that we see more. What we get is always more, and better, than what we see. Human beings put the best things first; God keeps the best to the end: we shall see him, as he is.

THE SWORD OF CHRIST

Sunday after Christmas day
ASB p.450

THE picture of Jesus that the evangelists present is not at all sentimental; they do not depict a character who is loved by all, or a life that is lived without opposition and tension. Of the four accounts in the gospels, it is Luke's that comes nearest to being the story of a hero, accepted by crowds; it is only in Luke that anyone goes with him to his execution, and there Jesus tells them not to weep for him, but for themselvers and their children (23.26–31). So Luke will not finish his account of the birth of Jesus without a prediction of the trouble that is to come. People will reject Jesus, Simeon says, and some will fall, and Mary's heart will be pierced: it will not be roses all the way (Luke 2.33–35).

Luke knew well how contentious Christian claims were, and in Acts he shows how synagogues were divided by the coming of the gospel, and cities and communities split into warring factions.

There has been a type of devotion to Jesus that has not taken account of his distance from us and ours from him, or of the negative aspects of his relationship with us. We have thought of him as the lover of our souls, and forgotten that love-affairs are often stormy.

Matthew brought the story of Herod and his plan to kill Jesus, into the introductory narratives of his gospel. Luke brings on Simeon and his predictions, for much the same purpose. We should not be deceived into thinking that faith will provide us with a smooth passage through life. Our secret thoughts will be laid bare: it is a word that usually means bad thoughts; Christ will provoke them in us. It may be the only way that he can get rid of them for us.

PRESENT GLORY

2nd after Christmas
ASB p.454

THERE is one aspect of Christian faith that the English find it hard to accept: the embarrassment of glory. We know that Christ's demands are unlimited in their scope; we know that he requires us to give up everything to follow him, and that there is no end to the humiliation that we shall have to endure for his sake. All this comes to us as no surprise. But what we had not expected, and had not been prepared for by our English upbringing, was the glory that he gives us. Not only glory in the age to come; we can accommodate ourselves to that; but glory now. Unlike some of our continental cousins, we are ill at ease with present glory.

An example of what makes us uncomfortable is that Jesus says to his followers, You are light for all the world (Matthew 5.14); and John, too, of the city to which we hope to belong, The glory of God gave it light (Revelation 21.23). We find it easier and more congenial to talk ourselves down, to be depreciatory about the church, and to draw attention to the faults and inadequacies in us and in it. It is more in accordance with our national outlook to disparage ourselves, than to believe in ourselves; and to believe in our present glory strikes us as impossible.

But this is what the prophet will tell us this Sunday:

> Arise, Jerusalem
> rise clothed in light; your light has come
> and the glory of the Lord shines over you.

It is there that the difference lies between what embarrasses us, and what we are to believe about ourselves. We are not required to believe in our own light or glory, or in the goodness of our lives. What will attract others, the prophet goes on to say, is nothing that is inherent in us – our power, our holiness. What we are required to believe in is the glory of the Lord that shines over us; or, as John puts it, the Lord is the lamp. We are light for all the world because Christ is the light of the world. We are more like the moon than the sun; our light is a reflection; the glory of the church is God's glory, seen as it were in a mirror.

When we say in the Creed that we believe in the church, we are asking God to strengthen our weak grasp of what it is we belong to. It is not this group of people that we can see and count; when we have added up the members we have not said anything about what they add up to. They are transformed into a different kind of society; their meetings are occasions of an entirely different sort. They are a large part of the evidence for the existence and activity of God. If we could see them as they really are, we would see God. At the ordination of priests, the Bishop used to say, The Church and Congregation whom you must serve, is his Spouse, and his Body. The prophecy has been fulfilled:

> The Lord shall shine upon you and over you shall his glory
>   appear;
> the nations shall march towards your light
> and their kings to your sunrise.

Epiphany
(*See Year One – Page 21*)

ONE THING I KNOW

1st after Epiphany
ASB p.463

JOHN the Baptist says that he has seen the Spirit coming upon Jesus, and borne witness; he could not have borne witness, had he not seen and thus had something to say, because witnessing is speaking, and speaking must have content if it is to be of any use.

The indissoluble connection between rational speech and content raises the awkward question, How can we bear witness? What do we have to say? What have we seen? If we can only be witnesses if we have something to which we can bear witness, then what is it?

It would misrepresent the mind of the fourth evangelist totally if we were to say, It all happened long ago, so there is no sense in which we can think of ourselves as witnesses; John the Baptist, on the other hand, was a contemporary of Jesus, so it was possible for him to say what he had seen; but we are not his contemporaries, therefore we cannot. When Jesus says in this gospel, You are my witnesses (15.27) he does not mean to restrict this to the first disciples only; they were witnesses because the Spirit came upon them; he comes upon us, too.

Nevertheless, that does not provide us with the answer to the question, What do we have to say? What have we seen? Suppose we said, there is the whole story of our redemption in the books of the Bible; there is the whole spread of Christine doctrine summarized in the creeds; and there are nearly two thousand years of the history of the church; there is no shortage of material; rather, the problem is that we have too much.

While that is true, it does not entirely deal with the problem. Recounting what other people have believed and said and done and suffered is not what is meant by bearing witness. There is more to being a witness than that. The witness has to declare the value of what he says, and this value must be of the highest order for what he says to be testimony. He must say, in effect, This is how it is, and I am willing to stake my life upon it. Other people have believed this, and some of them have died for it; I believe it too, and I hope that, if the situation arose, I would choose to die rather than deny it.

The length of the Bible, the vast area of Christian doctrine and the two millennia of church history should not frighten us off. We do not have to bear witness to it all. John the Baptist had only one thing to say: I have seen the Spirit coming upon Jesus. Later on in the gospel, the man who had been blind makes a single point: One thing I know: I was blind and now I see. The content of our testimony, that to which we can bear witness, may be very small indeed.

It is sometimes said of preachers, that though they may have preached hundreds, even thousands, of sermons in their lifetime, they have in fact only one, and all the others are variations on it. The same may be true of people who are not preachers: they have their own one piece of insight and conviction; it is the one thing that makes the whole of scripture, doctrine and church history valid for them.

Somebody said once that he could write his reason for being a believer on the back of a postage-stamp. That would be enough to make him a witness.

CALLED BY GOD

2nd after Epiphany
ASB p.467

WE can only describe faith to people who are willing to accept the possibility that what we believe in is true. This is why faith is such an odd and awkward thing, and why it is so difficult to give an account of it to anyone else. What believers feel compelled to say, if they are to speak at all adequately of their faith, is that the initiative did not lie with them; they did not decide to believe. The idea is expressed by the biblical writers when they use the word *call*.

It is one thing to volunteer. Then the initiative does lie with the person who offers to undertake the difficult, unpleasant job, or whatever it is. The more pressure is exerted from outside, the less it is an instance of volunteering. To make the wholly obvious point, to be said to volunteer you must be acting voluntarily – not under external compulsion or persuasion.

The opposite of volunteering is being selected, nominated, appointed. (Hence the joke: You, you, and you will volunteer.) Jesus calls disciples to follow him; Paul says, God called me. 'Those who are called' is one of the many descriptions that were used, before the word Christian was invented.

Sometimes the word *call* is used for inviting people to a party; then 'those who were called' means the guests. This brings out the meaning very clearly, since no one (we hope) would choose to go to a party without an invitation from the host. One would be thought odd if one said, I volunteered to attend the wedding-breakfast, had there been nothing of any description to request the pleasure of one's company.

Faith, discipleship, being a Christian, is a calling in the sense that it is not a matter of volunteering; it is a response to an invitation

– so the believer understands it – from God. The initiative does not lie with the believers, but with the one in whom they believe. They did not work it out for themselves; it was more like a present, out of the blue. This is what so often makes it difficult to explain one's reason for believing; whatever you say, you know that that's not the real thing.

If this is at all a true account of how it is, then one conclusion is immediately obvious. If it was not our idea in the first place that we should believe, then it must follow that thankfulness must have priority over everything else. First and last and above all, we thank God who has called us into this grace in which we now stand. It makes no difference how imperfect our obedience has been, or how weak our faith or non-existent our love; the fact is that we still have an inkling that there is a God, and we are grateful for that, and thank him for it. We could not have had it had he not given it to us. It does not feel like a discovery that we have made for ourselves; we do not want to congratulate ourselves. Its character is that of a gift, unexpected, unsolicited and undeserved.

Say, if you like, that it is a vicious circle; or that it is a virtuous circle: Faith requires belief in the object of faith before it can be understood and described. The way believers think of themselves is as those whom God has called, invited, summoned. Nothing less than that will express what it is they have to say about themselves.

NECESSARY HYPERBOLE

3rd after Epiphany
ASB p.471

THERE is a recklessness about Christianity, which cautious people must find disturbing. Was it really wise of Paul to say, There is nothing I cannot master? Is this not a recipe for falling into irresistible temptation? Would it not have been wiser and more humble, and would it not have shown more understanding of himself, if he had said that he had learnt how to cope with some situations in which he constantly found himself, but that there were others that continued to catch him out? – that he still had his weak and tender spots, and that if you mentioned them to him, he might blow his top; such as Judaizers, or knowledge, or women without veils?

But when you come to think about it, it is not only Paul who makes these reckless claims. Jesus does so too: Truly I tell you: if anyone says to this mountain, Be lifted from your place and hurled into the sea, and has no inward doubts, but believes that what he says will happen, it will be done for him (Mark 11.23). Again, Everything is possible for God (Mark 10.27).

It is an idea that has its roots in the writers of Hebrew history. The prime example is David and Goliath; but it is repeated again and again in the accounts of small (Hebrew) armies defeating large (gentile) armies. It is an important theme, for example, in the accounts of the Maccabean wars.

Prudence and caution are thrown to the wind, and total confidence takes their place. This confidence, however, is not self-confidence – it is not reliance on one's own ability; it is confidence in God. The whole sentence in the Letter to the Phillipians reads (in the Jerusalem Bible translation): There is nothing I cannot master with the help of the One who gives me strength (4.13). What Paul wrote, in Greek, was much shorter and crisper than that; it took him only six words to say it, and a literal translation would be: I am totally competent through the one who empowers me.

This way of talking about hurling mountains, unlimited possibilities and universal competence is called hyperbole. It is difficult to avoid it, in religion. The subject-matter seems to make it necessary. There is a parallel case in the field of love-letters. No-one would think of writing, You are the most beautiful person south of the Trent; or even, You are the most wonderful person I have met so far. Either of these would leave something unstated that should have been said. What one writes is, You are far and away the best person in the whole world. Nothing less than this will do.

Just as love has to be expressed in hyperbolic language, so also does faith. Prudence goes out through the window, when love and faith come in at the door.

NO SACRED PLACES

4th after Epiphany
ASB p.476

THE author of the fourth gospel uses blanket denials to emphasize what he wants to affirm. When Jesus says, You will worship the Father neither on this mountain nor in Jerusalem, we are not meant to think that there will never be any true worship of God in Samaria or in Judaea. The negative serves the positive, and the positive is that God can be worshipped everywhere; locality is of no more importance.

Of course it is true that some places are easier to pray in than others. We all have our private lists: Iona, Chartres, Assisi, etc. But this is a luxury we must learn to do without, because if we do not, if we depend on it, it will cease to be effective. Holy places are a bonus, a gift, a grace: and grace is never to be presumed upon.

The worshipper will worship the Father in spirit and truth: that is the kind of worshipper the Father wants (John 4.23). Spirit is here the opposite of place and building; churches in the sense of buildings were a development much later than the time of the writers of the New Testament; none of them would ever have had the experience of worshipping God in a church (in the sense we use the word now). Truth is Christ, who abides in the believer, and the believer is in him. This new order is the work of God, who establishes what he wants. The time of sacred places and sacred buildings is over.

But the only reason for saying this is to emphasize the opposite; the only point of being an iconoclast is to assert the real presence of God. We do not need ritual, ceremony, sacred place, or any of the other visible and tangible expressions of religion in order to be with God. He is in close proximity with us, wherever we are; we can turn to him at any moment and in any place. One way to affirm this is to deny our dependence on everything else.

5th after Epiphany
(*See Year One – Page 28*)

6th after Epiphany
(*See Year One – Page 30*)

THE FRUITFULNESS OF THE WORD

9th before Easter
ASB p.486

To speak of a seed yielding a hundredfold is to exaggerate; so the authorities on this subject say. But the exaggeration is deliberate and significant, pointing emphatically to the rich productivity of God. We reckon national growth-rates in single-figure percentages; if we were to express the parabolic seed's fertility in this way it would be ten thousand per cent. The hyperbole is meant to make us stop and think.

We are dealing with a God who is not to be thought of as ancient of days, dried up and withered; or as one who is merely passive and receptive, accepting the praises of heaven and earth. He is, as the interpretation of the parable says, one whose word brings forth fruit in those who hear it and hold it fast. He is the author of all good works, and these are immense and unmeasurable both in quantity and in quality.

Anyone who has ever had the slightest faith in God knows that this is so. They know that they have done things they would not have dared to do without faith, and that they have endured situations that would have broken them completely had they not believed that, in some inexplicable way, God was in control, or would be one day.

It is not just that God inspires and motivates human goodness; he also purifies what is unclean in our actions and makes perfect what we know to be very imperfect. The full range of our faults is concealed from others (as it is also in part from ourselves), in order that what we do may not be spoiled for them at its source in our half-heartedness and self-centredness. God over-rides our failure. People are less critical of us than they might be, and accept from us more than we had intended to give and better than we could provide.

God is the author of all goodness, of all the kind, loving, helpful and constructive actions that have ever been done in the world. He is like a stream of water that never varies because it flows from a spring that never fails. He can be relied upon to begin and continue and complete good works in the world he has made, through the people he has made. There is no reason why we should behave in a positive, loving, self-sacrificing way to one another, except the fruitfulness of God who directs and sustains all such activity. This continuing human goodness should not be taken for granted, as though we had any right to expect it. On the contrary, we have every right to expect rivalry, competitiveness, destruction and all the negative attitudes that spring from our faulty wills.

What in fact happens is better than anyone could have dared to hope for, and it happens because we are not in charge of ourselves, or of our actions, or of the effects of our actions. All these are the result of the goodness of God and his productivity is infinite.

THE GOSPEL AND ITS MINISTERS

8th before Easter
ASB p.490

IT would be strange and disturbing to find yourself a member of a party in a restaurant, and all the conversation was about the waiters and the waitresses. Yet this is what has happened. There is now, and has been for centuries, far more discussion, disagreement and division among Christians over ministry than over what it is that is to be ministered – the gospel.

The comparison with meals and waiters is fair, and invites itself for consideration, because the words that the first Greek-speaking Christians used for ministry were the words for serving meals, handing out dishes and waiting at table. There is an example of the literal sense in John's account of the wedding at Cana: the mother of Jesus speaks to the waiters, and it is the waiters who know where the good wine has come from. (Literally translated, they are 'the deacons' John 2.5,9.) Again, when Jesus heals Peter's mother-in-law after the sabbath synagogue service, the miracle is confirmed by the fact that she can wait on the men, helping to dish out the supper (Mark 1.31).

Controversy about ministry started early, and some of 1 Corinthians and most of 2 Corinthians are about it. Paul believed that God was opposed to such quarrels and disputes, and that God had deliberately arranged things so that divisions on this issue would not happen. Paul's thorn in the flesh has been discussed at length but nobody knows for certain what it was; all we do know (and all we need to know) is that it was unpleasant for Paul, that it humiliated him before other people, and that he had prayed three times for it to be removed. In the end, however, he had come to believe that the condition, whatever it was (physical or mental), was there for a purpose: to stop him from being too proud, and to prevent others from having too high an opinion of him.

In the ancient world it would have counted against the truth of the gospel that its messengers were accident-prone and suffered from physical disabilities. (See Galatians 4.12–14.) Religion was expected to cure its devotees of such disadvantages and to protect them from humiliation. Paul sees it the other way round: God picks on the least likely people to be his agents, so that the power may be seen to be Christ's, not theirs; and it is Christ crucified, powerless. The message is what matters, not the medium through which it comes; or rather, the medium must be like the message.

There is something here for everybody. For those who hold any kind of office in the church: they are more effective the more disastrous their lives. For those who are being waited upon by them (the guests): God has deliberately arranged matters so that we should expect nothing else but the weakness of the clergy; he meant them to be the butt of insult and to suffer hardship, persecution, agony. It is when they are weak that they are strong; when no one thinks well of them that they are most effective in their work.

YOUR SINS ARE FORGIVEN

7th before Easter
ASB p.495

THOSE most comforting words, The Lord has put away your sins, have been taken from us in the more recent translations of the Bible; the REB, for example, has: the Lord has laid on another the consequences of your sin . . . the child who will be born to you shall die (2 Samuel 12.13f). This is, indeed, exactly what we expect. We live in a world that is unremitting; where effect follows cause without mercy; and we take our cue from it and expect our faults and mistakes to be dealt with by others, as they see fit. God, we assume, is like everybody else, only more so; his honour must be maintained, therefore there have to be procedures for dealing with sin that secure the holiness of his name – sacrifice, or almsgiving, or repentance. Whatever the method is, it means that something must be done by the sinner to put the relationship right; and God has revealed what this is.

Forgiveness, on the other hand, is different. The person who forgives asks for nothing and expects nothing from the one who is being forgiven. This never happens in the natural order; there may be temporary remission of a disease, but it is only temporary; in the end, everything dies. The wages of sin is death.

It is because it is so unlike nature, that it is hard to believe in the forgiveness of sins, which John the Baptist and Jesus after him, both proclaimed – Jesus being more radical than even John and acquiring for himself from his opponents the title, A friend of tax-collectors and sinners (Matthew 11.19).

Good news is always hard to accept. People say, I don't believe it! Tell me again, what did you say? Could I possibly have it in writing, so that I can feel it and handle it for myself?

It is difficult to believe in forgiveness, and difficult to accept it, or to assure others that they have been forgiven. Is this, perhaps, the church's main and most puzzling task? We all prefer to hang on to our guilt, rather than believe that God has completely removed it, like a tape that has been wiped off.

The story of the woman caught committing adultery (notice that her partner in the act is never mentioned; but it takes two to do it) is not part of the fourth gospel, but is part of the New Testament; it was preserved for the sake of the final saying of Jesus: Nor do I condemn you. You may go; do not sin again (John 8.11). It would be a total mistake to think that the words, Do not sin again, expressed the condition on which the statement, Nor do I condemn you, depended; as though Jesus meant, If you do it again, then I really shall condemn you, and for both occasions, too. When forgiveness is accepted it creates in the person forgiven the will and intention never to do it again. There are no conditions. (How unfortunate it is that the ASB uses the expression, Almighty God, who forgives all who truly repent – inviting us to doubt the genuineness of our repentance, and therefore the truth of our forgiveness.)

Forgiveness is undeserved, unexpected, unearned. It is like a miracle. O happy chance!

Ash Wednesday
(*See Year One – Page 36*)

TESTING GOD

1st in Lent
ASB p.503

LUKE has the temptation to put God to the test as the last of the three and the climax of the series (Luke 4.9–12). This is the one we are most likely to fall for, because of the climate of the time in which we live.

We have learnt to trust machines in a way that our predecessors could hardly have imagined. If, only a few years ago, you had told me that by the 1990's I would be getting my cash from a hole in the wall by means of a bit of plastic and a secret number, I should never have believed you; and it is still such a new experience that it has not yet lost its surprise: will it work again, this time? Try it and see; it usually does. We have learnt to trust cashpoints, cars, telephones, radios . . . the list is vast. And if you have any doubt, the answer is always, Try it and see if it works; this is the one test and it is completely sufficient.

So should I trust God, and see if he is as reliable as a machine? Or perhaps even more reliable, because machines occasionally break down, but he will never do so. Should I make my requests known to God, with thanksgiving, confident that he will answer me; and should I expect the answers to come, exactly as I had framed them?

The confusion arises because we ought to be using faith in different senses; faith in machines is not the same as faith in God (or faith in our friends). This is why the appropriate tests are different in each case. Machines are tested by results that can be predicted; if we treat our friends like that, we find that we are losing them fast. And it is much the same with God: we shall not build up reasons to believe in him, by putting him to the test. Elijah on Mount Carmel is not the model for us to follow (1 Kings 18).

Ironically it was a sixteenth century Carmelite, who believed that his Order had been founded by Elijah, who also taught with extreme clarity that our goal, union with God by faith, annihilates the understanding. There will be less and less for our minds to think about, the nearer we come to believing in God. The only result we should expect is the absence of results. The idea is there also in other parts of the Old Testament and the New. For example:

> The fig tree has no buds,
> The vines bear no harvest,
> The olive crop fails,
> The orchards yield no food,
> The fold is bereft of its flock,
> and there are no cattle in the stalls.
> Even so I shall exult in the Lord
> and rejoice in the God who saves me (Habakkuk 3.17f).

> Abba, Father, all things are possible to you;
> take this cup from me.
> Yet not my will but yours (Mark 14.36).

> To see something is no longer to hope (Romans 8.24).

God wants us for ourselves; and he wants us to want him for himself (not his gifts). We shall need to have an exacting faith and hope and love, that will do without instant results to re-assure us. The sufficient success upon earth for which we pray is a diminishing quantity, fast approaching zero.

SCATTERING AND GATHERING

2nd in Lent
ASB p.508

THE contrasting words, gather and scatter (Matthew 12.30), belong to talk about sheep and shepherds; in John's gospel, it is the wolf that scatters the sheep; the shepherd's task, on the other hand, is to bring them together, so that not one of them is lost. The choice that everybody has to make is whether to be a gatherer or a scatterer – one who brings people together, out of their isolation and distrust, or one who adds to the divisions that are there already in our society, and increases mutual fear and suspicion.

The saying of Jesus, however, contains more than the bare contrast between the only possible alternatives; he says, He who does not gather *with me* scatters (Matthew 12.30). He speaks of himself as one who is a gatherer, and he invites others to join him in this activity.

But there are other sayings of Jesus in the gospels, in which he says that he has come to bring division to families; not peace but a sword. So the problem is, how to reconcile the divisiveness of Jesus (which has continued among his followers) with his statement here that he is a gatherer.

It cannot be denied that both elements are found in the gospels, and that both activities happen to his followers. There are predictions that his disciples will be hated and put to death, and it has happened again and again. There are promises that Christ will be lifted up and draw everyone to himself, and this too has happened; he has broken down divisions and healed the wounds that we have inflicted on one another.

A good case could be made out for the view that some people are, by temperament or circumstances, more drawn to one aspect of Jesus than the other. Matthew, for example, builds his whole book on the theme of divisions, from Herod and the magi, at the beginning, to parables of wise and foolish brides-maids, good and bad servants, sheep and goats, in chapter 25; and finally to the Jews who think that the body was taken away by the disciples and the eleven who are commissioned by Jesus on the mountain. And yet it is Matthew who has the saying, He who does not gather with me ... Paul is an example of one who frequently stresses the universality of Christ's work: As in Adam all die, so in Christ all will be brought to life (1 Corinthians 15.22); in shutting all mankind in the prison of their disobedi-ence, God's purpose was to show mercy to all mankind (Romans 11.32). Paul, for all his experience of rejection and persecution, believed in Christ as the one who gathers together everything that God has made.

This may be the solution of the problem, How can Jesus be both a scatterer and a gatherer? How can he both divide and unite? The divisions are temporary; the uniting is in the future, and eter-nal. The last thing that the Son of man will do, according to Mark, is to gather (13.27). We shall have to bear with our unhappy divisions in the belief that they will be healed by Christ in the end.

HOW HAVE I DONE?

3rd in Lent
ASB p.512

THERE is more about rewards in Matthew's gospel than in all the other three put together; it is a theme that he emphasises heavily. For example, the teaching about discipleship in Matthew that comes in today's gospel (16.24–28) has close parallels in

Mark and Luke but it is only Matthew who has the saying, He will reward each one according to his behaviour. (The words are closely similar to Psalm 62.12.)

Matthew's strong and frequent reference to future rewards embarrasses us, in much the same way that money and salaries are not quite proper topics for conversation in some parts of our society. Moreover, it is regarded as slightly quaint and old-fashioned (or jokey) to say of someone who has died, that they have gone to their reward.

When one begins to look into it, the problem is worse than it might at first appear; Matthew has no doubt that not all rewards will be welcomed by those who receive them. The saying, He will reward each one according to his behaviour, means not only that he will give good things to the faithful, but also that he will punish the wicked. It could be translated, He will pay each according to their performance. The final sections of the last discourse depict the judgement of the believers (the servants) and the judgement of the unbelievers (the sheep and the goats), and in both cases, some go to joy and others to sorrow.

Would it help us to think about this and to overcome our prejudice against this topic that is so prominent in Matthew, if we were to approach it from a different angle? Most of the time, if not all the time, we live and act in total ignorance about ourselves. Even if we pause to reflect on what we are doing, we scarcely know what our motives are, or what it is that is driving us. Occasionally there are flashes of insight, but it is a question how closely we attend to them; there are bursts of anger, or feelings of deep disappointment which offer us opportunities for greater self-awareness, yet we seldom feel we have understood them. It is one of those situations in which the more you know, the more you know that you do not know. Shall we ever find out what has been the truth about ourselves?

Could it be that Matthew's insistence on the theme of rewards and punishments at the last judgement, when this life is ended (an insistence that is almost unparalleled in the rest of the New Testament) is to be seen as a benefit to be welcomed, rather than an embarrassment to be regretted? We shall find out the truth about ourselves, at last.

If there is the life of the world to come (as the Creed says), then a complete and authorative assessment of what we have done will be inevitable and necessary and is to be welcomed. We could not want to live an eternal lie, posturing on for eternity as we have done here.

There are two points to hang on to. The first is that it would be immature to avoid the question, How have I done? The second is that it is possible to dare to ask it, because we believe that our assessor is merciful. The Psalm that Matthew is alluding to ends as follows:

> One thing God has spoken,
> two things have I learnt:
> 'Power belongs to God'
> and 'Unfailing love is yours, Lord';
> you reward everyone according to what he has done.

LISTEN TO HIM

4th in Lent
ASB p.517

THE chief point of the story of the transfiguration is in the final words of the voice from the bright cloud, Listen to him (Matthew 17.5). This is what the three disciples are to tell the rest of the followers of Jesus, after the resurrection; the church will live through listening to him.

If this is so, then it should be possible, even in a few hundred words, to say what it is that Jesus says; and however difficult it is to do this, and however mistaken any one attempt may be (must be), there is still an obligation to try to do it.

He proclaims the coming rule of God; that means that we live in a world that is not right as it is: and that we must long for it to be different. We are to want justice for all, better conditions, a richer and fuller life for everybody. The will of God is that he should reign everywhere in his creation, and that every kind of evil should be abolished.

Along with his proclamation of a world-wide reformation he requires also a change in the minds of his followers and, eventually, of everybody. The evil that must be removed from them is their concern for themselves, which shows in the way they treat one another, and in what they think about money and property. They think of themselves as centres of importance, and they provide themselves with security by owning things and influencing people. They act as though events must happen in the way that will serve their purposes. But this is not how life really is, or how it was meant to be, or how it ever will be. There is only one God, and he is the centre of everything, and will in the end be seen as such. The one maker will also be the only ruler.

God's purpose is to make this happen in every thing and in every place. But this must not be thought of as a threat to the well-being of his creatures; that would be a complete misunderstanding. His will that everything should change is part of his desire that everything should come to its intended goal and become what he has always meant it to be. God will see that this happens; to resist, is to resist one's own good, and that is absurd, tragic and probably, in the end, impossible.

So, although the cost of being a follower of Jesus is total (death, and resurrection) what is offered is without price. Everything must be abandoned, for everything. Or rather since our idea of everything that we have and can control is a mistake, nothing is abandoned (except the illusion of owning) and everything is promised to us.

So long as we stand outside, this looks like bad news; the insiders, however, those who have taken the first steps, know that the news is very good.

HE GAVE HIMSELF UP

5th in Lent
ASB p.521

THE Son of Man did not come to be served, but to serve; and he did this, by giving up his life. We can best approach this, if we start from the bare statement that is made in the Apostles' Creed: He died.

There was nothing to be gained by inventing the story of a saviour who had been put to death. Paul said that a crucified person was an offence to Jews and folly to gentiles; and he had every reason to know, because not only had he preached it to Jews and gentiles, but he had himself also known Christ after the flesh – that is, as one who was an offence and whose followers, he believed, should be persecuted and destroyed.

Although we cannot reconstruct the circumstances surrounding the death of Jesus (e.g. what the charge was on which he was condemned; who took the initiative), nevertheless the evidence, such as it is, points to the willingness of Jesus not to resist execution.

That Jesus accepted death as the consequence of his life has had its effect upon all his followers. Their attitude to life and the pattern of their behaviour have been formed and influenced by his death, understood as the voluntary surrender of his life. We only need to ask the question, What would it have been like to be a follower of Jesus if the arrest had not led to the crucifixion? Suppose Jesus had run away before Judas identified him to those whom he had brought with him to Gethsemane; or that Jesus had argued with the chief priests, or with Pilate, and persuaded them to release him, and then lived another thirty years and died of old age in his bed. We should have had to think of him in an entirely different way. We might have admired him for his resourcefulness and the skill with which he had saved his life; it is more likely that we should never have heard of him at all. No one could have written of him that he fulfilled Zechariah's prophecy, I will strike the shepherd and the sheep will be scattered (Mark 14.27). No one could have described him as saying, If I am the man you want, let these others go (John 18.8). Nor could anyone have attributed to him the saying, I lay down my life for the sheep (John 10.15). Paul could never have written, He loved me and gave himself up for me (Galatians 2.20).

One way in which we can understand how it was that the Son of Man had to be put to death (Mark 8.31) is this: If faith is to be trust in one who is wholly for us, without any reservation on his part, or hesitation on ours, then it is difficult to see how this kind of faith could be elicited other than by a death that was accepted voluntarily. The first three gospels tell the story of Gethsemane in order to make this point; and even in the fourth gospel, which does not have the story, there is still the saying of Jesus, The cup that the Father has given me, surely I must drink it? (John 18.11).

THE KING WHO COMES IN GENTLENESS

Palm Sunday
ASB p.526

THE more you read the gospels, the more surprising their authors turn out to be. They refuse to be fitted into the pigeon-holes to which we had at first assigned them. Matthew, for example, seems initially to be the evangelist who goes furthest in the direction of attempting to objectify the truth of the story he is telling; he describes the events in his book in such a way that the reader feels it must be true and it would be ridiculous not to believe it. If this is what happened, then of course I must assent to it – from the miraculous star at the beginning, bringing astrologers from the east, to earthquakes and a resurrection of many saints and their appearance in Jerusalem at the end, not to mention an angel of the Lord seen by the guard and reported by them to the chief priests. Matthew, we feel, is bullying us into faith; are we free to refuse to be persuaded?

But then we come upon something else in Matthew's gospel, and only in Matthew's. It is important to him, and yet it is the exact opposite of what we took to be his hectoring attitude. 'Gentle' is not a word that we would have used to describe this writer; more likely we would have called him violent, aggressive. But 'gentle' is a word he uses three times, and he is the only evangelist to introduce it into his gospel. Twice he describes Jesus as gentle (11.29 and 21.5) and it is, he says, the gentle who will possess the earth when God's kingdom comes (5.5).

It is only to disciples that Jesus appears and reveals himself as the one who has all authority in heaven and on earth. There are no appearances of the risen Lord to unbelievers, to Caiaphas or to Pilate (or even to Pilate's wife). Matthew knows that God will

134

not force us into faith (how could he?) but will respect the freedom of his creatures. We may think that Matthew has almost exceeded the limit, but his intention is only to persuade us, not to compel.

Jesus is gentle, not violent; he shows it, Matthew writes, by the way in which he entered Jerusalem: Here is your king, who comes to you in gentleness, riding on an ass, riding on the foal of a beast of burden.

Only the strong can be gentle; the weak cannot. The only course open to the weak is the use of force. But those who are strong can control themselves, be patient, be long-suffering, wait for opportunities to develop, bide their time. This is the character of Jesus, as Matthew had come to know him, and as he presents him to us today.

Maundy Thursday
(*See Year One – Page 45*)

Good Friday
(*See Year One – Page 46*)

EVERYTHING IS POSSIBLE

Easter Day
ASB p.573

THE women were wondering among themselves who would roll away the stone from the entrance to the tomb; but then they looked up and saw that it had been rolled back already; it was a very large stone, too. This is the first hint that Mark gives us in his account of Easter day (16.3f) that the course of it is not going to be in accordance with human, unbelieving expectations; there will not be a dead Jesus, or an anointing, or a return to things as they had been in the past – fishing in the lake, mending nets, suppers served by Peter's mother-in-law. It is at this point in Mark's story that we are made to think for the first time that the future will be entirely different from what the women were thinking it would be: the stone, which they had seen Joseph roll against the entrance, was now rolled back, contrary to their expectations, and the young man in a white robe told them what had happened: God has raised Jesus, that is why he is not here. Mark finishes off his gospel with the description of the women's fear, amazement and silence.

The God who prevents us in all our doings with his most gracious favour is always doing things like this, and catching us out in our unbelief. The women should have believed what Jesus had said so frequently, that he had to rise again after three days; but they had not understood, or attended to what he was saying. They had thought (as we think) that the present and the future are the product of the past; that there is no new thing under the sun; that whether a tree falls south or north, it must lie as it falls. They thought (as we think) that God does nothing, and that impossible situations are simply impossible.

Mark wants to tell us that it is not so. He has a sentence he repeats in his book, it is so important to him, and to our understanding of his message – it is the key to the whole story:

Everything is possible to one who believes (9.23).
Everything is possible for God (10.27)
Abba Father, everything is possible to you (14.36).

Our continuing unbelief is put to shame by God. We think we shall not be able to cope, and then we find that we have done so. Our lives are long lists of moments of unbelief, followed by divine surprises of love, joy, peace and all the rest of the fruit of the Spirit.

It would be a mistake to define resurrection as though it were entirely an event in the past, on the first Easter day. What happened then is what happens again and again: God reverses our expectations; joy breaks in; the impossible becomes possible. We believe in the resurrection of Jesus after three days, because we know God as the one who raises us from despair to life, day after day. If we had not known it in our own lives, we should never have believed it of him.

THE ACTION OF GOD

1st after Easter
ASB p.602

THE bread that we need in order to live the real life (the life of God) is Jesus; the only way to have this bread, John believes, is to have Jesus. He who possesses the Son possesses life (1 John 5.12). To have Jesus is to come to him, which is the same as to believe in him. That seems clear enough; let us then believe. But John will not allow us to stop there; the act of believing is more complicated than we had thought; it is not the result of a simple decision: shall I do this, or that? The believers are a gift which the Father gives to the Son; there is this action from God to God, before there can be any human decision; it is the action of God that makes the human decision possible.

The Johannine theology is puzzling, and leaves us with disturbing questions but no answers to them: Does the Father give only some people to the Son, not everybody? Why are there any who are left out? Are the unbelievers not responsible for their unbelief? We might say that John's way of thinking raises more questions than it answers; and if we do, we are then left with the problem, What questions does it answer? Perhaps the one and only question to which this Johannine theology provides an answer is, Why did I believe in the first place, and why do I find myself continuing to believe; why have I not given up? John is concerned with the mystery of the persistence of faith.

When John writes: All that the Father gives me will come to me (6.37); and, That I should lose nothing of all that he has given to me (6.39), he uses the singular neuter adjective, literally: the one whole thing that the Father gives. The believers, all of them together, form just one thing. This rebukes us, for a start. We had thought of ourselves as individuals taking decisions on our own; and that faith was a private matter, a choice we made in isolation from others. John is pointing to a different aspect of faith; we are tied up with others, part of a collective, united with all the believers of the past, the present and the future, as one single object.

What we are is the gift of the Father to the Son. What we experience as our decision to believe, to trust in Christ, is not simply that; it is the result of something that is going on outside us − before we were born and apart from our choices. God's action comes first, and it is the ground of our believing.

It is not easy to think of an analogy; but, for what it is worth, it is somewhat like this: We were born into a world that is in motion, turning on itself and circling the sun. We go with the earth and seldom think of its motion, except when we have time to watch shadows moving across gardens and streets. Day and night, and the seasons of the year, happen to us, whether we want them to do so or not. (Jesus says in this passage that he does not do his own will, but the will of the one who sent him.) We cannot choose when the flowers in the garden will bloom or the trees have their leaves. The continuance of our faith is also apart from our decision; indeed it, like all our good deeds, is wrought in God (John 3.21).

OTHER SHEEP

2nd after Easter
ASB p.607

WHO are the other sheep who do not belong to this fold? The commentators usually say they are the gentiles, and that this fold means Judaism; gentiles will listen to the good shepherd's voice, and he will bring them in, to become part of the one flock under the one shepherd.

If that is the way to read this passage, then what is foretold in this gospel has already happened, in that the church includes gentiles; they are, in fact, the majority. What follows from this is that the prediction that there will be other sheep from elsewhere ceases to have any great significance for us: Oh yes, we say (if we happen to be gentiles), it refers to us; we are these other sheep.

There is not much in the rest of John's gospel that suggests that he was concerned with the difference between Jews and gentiles, apart from the Greeks in chapter 12. So maybe we are restricting the force of the saying about other sheep not of this fold, by confining it to one interpretation when it may have a wider application.

Those of us who were brought up on the BCP expect today's gospel to end with the words: one fold, one shepherd; we are surprised to find: one flock, one shepherd. Apparently all the Greek manuscripts have: one flock; the word *fold* here comes from Jerome's Latin translation; and it is often said that it is a sign of the weakness of our faith that we emphasize the external, visible and formal (*fold*), rather than the inward and spiritual (*flock*).

In much the same way, it is less disturbing to think that the saying about other sheep refers to people who are now safely within the flock (gentiles; ourselves), than to think that Jesus still has other sheep who are not within the church (a word which John does not use in the gospel). Would it not be more in accordance with the tenor of this writer, if we thought that what is being said here is being said to make us think: we have to do with a shepherd who has other concerns; there are other sheep; not just us?

It is Jesus who is the good shepherd, not the Ecumenical Patriarch, or the Pope, or the Archbishop of Canterbury, or any officer of any church; and he is not concerned only with those who believe themselves to be his sheep. He is always the shepherd who has other sheep that are not yet of this flock. We cannot draw boundaries; if we ever do, as someone said, Jesus is always on the other side of the line.

People who have nothing to do with any church still respond to generosity and self-forgetful goodness. There are sheep who listen to the voice of the good shepherd, the one who lays down his life for the sheep. Perhaps the reason why they do not belong to our fold is because they do not hear his voice when we speak; they do not hear the Hanged Man, and they will not listen to the voice of strangers.

LOOK AT THE EVIDENCE

3rd after Easter
ASB p.612

IN the Hebrew Scriptures, there is frequent appeal to the evidence: the way that you know what is true is through what you can actually see. Faith requires evidence, and God is willing to provide it; it would be perverse to ignore him. So the widow in Zarephath says that she now knows that Elijah is a man of God and that the Lord really speaks through him, only when the prophet has prayed for her son's life to be restored and God has answered his prayer (1 Kings 17.24).

Martha has the same sort of faith in Jesus: he would not have let Lazarus die if he had been present; he had healed the officer's boy and the lame man; and even now, God will answer his prayer. That is as far as she has got; what she has not yet understood is that Jesus is the resurrection, and that to believe in him is to have life in such a way that one will never die. Jesus performs the sign of the raising of Lazarus in order to provide the evidence for the faith that he is the resurrection.

We do not have the sign repeated for us; there are not annual resuscitations. We have John's book (in order that you may believe, 20.31), and the book shows us what to look for, because we have other evidence also. The book by itself would not convince us; it is the book as showing us where to look that is convincing. The other evidence to which it points is in our lives: they bear witness to us that Jesus is the resurrection.

This is the reason why we must examine our lives and scrutinize them to see what is there, in them; not take them for granted, but take them apart and look more closely at what goes on, every day. It is always better than it should be; there's always more to it than we deserve. People forgive us, and put up with our quirks, and love us in spite of our faults; there is no reason why we should be accepted – we find ourselves difficult enough to accept. We receive new energy to do things, although we have squandered what we had in the past; and new insights, although we have failed to act on the old ones. It is as though there were no one keeping the score against us, and the only thing that counted was the pluses.

Our life lies hidden with Christ in God. But the apostle would not say so, unless he meant us to take note of it; he does not want the fact that our life is hidden with Christ to go unnoticed by us. He wants us to see what is going on: that we are involved with Christ, and he with us; though it is hidden, we must look at it. It is because we are involved with Christ that things are better than we had any right to expect; it is because of him that black marks do not count against us, and the final black mark, the last negative, is death. Life is not fair, laddie (as the Scottish nanny said); it is biased, in our favour. This is the evidence that Jesus is the resurrection and the life.

WELCOME GUESTS

4th after Easter
ASB p.617

Have I been all this time with you, and you still do not know me? – The question that Jesus asks Philip, he could as well ask us, with even more reason for the surprise and rebuke that the question implies; we have, generally, had longer than Philip to find out who he is. Moreover we have the book in which Philip is the character who asks the question, and this book is designed to deal with Philip's request: Show us the Father and we ask no more. John's gospel is the answer to anyone who speaks like that.

The deeds of Jesus are the deeds of the Father, since the principal and his agent are one. The Son is wholly dependent on the Father, and does only what the Father has sent him to do. What the Father does is what the Son does also, and we can see this in the seven signs that give structure to the first half of the book. In these signs, God's action is always life-giving and creative: the absence of wine is turned into an embarrassing quantity of the best quality; the officer's son is brought back from the edge of death; the man who had been lame at the pool for thirty-eight years gets up and walks; there is more than enough food for five thousand; safety for the frightened disciples in the boat; a man born blind sees, and a dead man walks out of his tomb.

As the Father has life in himself, so by his gift the Son also has life in himself (5.26) and this life he gives to whom he wills. In John there are no herds of swine rushing down the slopes to be destroyed in the lake, nor is there any fig-tree that is cursed; all the signs of Jesus in this gospel are acts of restoration, enhancement, fulfilment. Destruction and condemnation are what we bring upon ourselves: God is the giver of good gifts and of nothing else except good gifts.

John bears witness to one who has done everything to show us the Father, and we need not ask him to do anything else. If we have read John's book and still do not know the Father, we have missed the point of the book. The aim of the book is to teach that God is wholly good and entirely for us; he is pure light without any darkness, the maker who does not destroy what he has made; unimaginable goodness, beyond our capacity to appreciate him, because our minds are too small and our hearts too confined.

We might say of a picture, I quite like it, but I would not want it in my house; I could not live with it; or of a person, I could not imagine living with him in the same place; he is all right for a bit. It is not so with God: the Father's house has many rooms, and Jesus brings us into them; God wants us to be close to him; he seeks us, and wants us to be one with him.

What we have wrongly supposed about the awe and majesty of

God has to be dismantled, because it gets in the way of what the Christian faith is really about; namely, the intention of God to associate us with himself in the closest and most intimate way. We are not to be servants, but guests – guests who have a permanent place in the Father's house.

JOY AND SORROW

5th after Easter
ASB p.622

BOTH the epistle and the gospel for this Sunday raise the question of the relationship between sorrow and joy. Our first thought might be to say that they are opposites, like hot and cold, or big and little. Opposites can only follow one another; they cannot exist together at the same time. So, for example, with sorrow and joy:

> Heaviness may endure for a night
> but joy comes in the morning (Psalm 30.5).

Hence the comparison in the gospel between the disciples and the woman having a baby: when the birth is over, she forgets the anguish in her joy; and similarly the disciples are sad on Friday, but Jesus will see them on Sunday, and grief will be turned to joy.

But perhaps it is Paul who has the deeper insight into the relationship between sorrow and joy. Those things that might be thought to cause sorrow, do so no longer: tribulation, persecution, famine, nakedness, peril, sword. Paul knows, because being an apostle is continual exposure to destruction; it is being killed all the day long; it is like being a sheep at the slaughterhouse. But, he says, in all these things we are more than conquerors. What to others would be occasions for sorrow, are now so no longer; they are the opposite: occasions for joy.

Or we could say, joy and sorrow are not mutually exclusive. Each needs the other, and they exist together; they are like birds in air or fish in water. The reason why this is so is because God has shown that he works for good in everything (Romans 8.28). There is nothing that is not grist to his mill; there is nothing that is unusable. He has taken our rejection of Christ and the crucifixion, and made it into the means of our salvation. He takes the weakness of the apostle, and uses it to reveal his own power more perfectly. He provides us with joy, in the very things that make us sad; because we can always say, God is working for good, even in this, that makes me sad.

Paul leads us to see that joy and sorrow are not opposites, like hot and cold, big and little, They do not exclude one another, but they can co-exist in the same person and at one time. Either is endangered if the other is not present: we are not ready yet for unmitigated joy; and too much sorrow would destroy us.

All the situations we find ourselves in have this double quality: there is that which makes us sad, and that which makes us rejoice; and both are there at the same time. We would not be experiencing the situation fully if we thought it was either wholly joyful, or wholly sad. Paul's word is more-than-conquerors, and conquering implies something to be overcome. Our joy and our sadness relate to the conflict in which we inevitably find ourselves, here and now. In the end, no doubt, it will be entirely different.

> Now in the meanwhile, with hearts raised on high,
> We for that country must yearn and must sigh;
> Seeking Jerusalem, dear native land,
> Through our long exile on Babylon's strand.

Ascension Day
(See Year One – Page 54)

REFLECTED GLORY

Sunday after Ascension Day
ASB p.629

L UKE's gospel ends where it had begun, in the temple, in Jerusalem. It started with Zechariah offering the incense; it ends with the disciples returning from Bethany to Jerusalem full of joy; and they were continually in the temple praising God.

The difference between the end of Matthew's gospel and the end of Luke's could hardly be more striking. There is nothing in Matthew about a departure of Jesus; on the contrary, the Lord who has now received all authority in heaven and on earth promises to be with his disciples all the days until the end of the age (28.20).

In Luke, Jesus withdraws from the disciples and they return to Jerusalem while he ascends to God's right hand. Luke therefore stresses the absence of Christ, where Matthew had drawn attention to his presence.

But to say that is too simple and to miss the point. The ascension and absence of Jesus, in Luke, is not a cause for distress, and is not described as though it were. Luke says that Jesus lifted up his hands and blessed the disciples; that they worshipped him, and were full of joy; and they praised God. Luke does not mean his readers to understand ascension as separation: Jesus has spoken of sending down what the Father promised; the disciples, he says, will be clothed with the power from on high. The ascension is something to rejoice about, according to Luke (who is the only writer in the New Testament who identifies it as a separate event from the resurrection, apart from a hint in that direction in John 20). It means, for one thing, that Jesus had been right in what he had said and done. He had brought forgiveness and invited sinners to repent and assured the thief that both of them would go to Paradise together. God had approved of

Jesus, and had demonstrated this by raising him to sit at his right hand, in fulfilment of the Psalm. This was God's way of showing that Jesus was his agent, and had spoken the truth; the ascension was God's seal of approval on the ministry of Jesus.

There was something else about the ascension that we find harder to appreciate, because we think of it as Christ's return to the Father. Luke, so far as we can tell, had no idea of a pre-existent divine being, who descended from God before he returned to God. As far as we know, Luke thought of Jesus as a man who had a mother, and whose life began at his conception. The ascension therefore, to Luke, was Christ's first entry into heaven, not his return; and it was a triumphant entry, because he was to be placed next to God.

To Luke, the idea to be stressed was that God had exalted one of us, a human being, the one who had been born at Bethlehem and brought up at Nazareth; we could bask in the reflected glory of the ascension of a fellow-member of the human race. This is why he describes the disciples as returning to Jerusalem full of joy, and praising God in the temple.

FILLED WITH THE SPIRIT

Pentecost
ASB p.634

WE can see the work that the Holy Spirit is doing in us and the effect that he has upon our lives; the only problem is to know what to look for. It is quite unnecessary, for example, to feel inferior to people who tell us that they have had some dramatic experience; there is no need, and it would be wrong, to write oneself off as a second-class Christian, because one did not speak with tongues or perform healings. There is a form of moral blackmail about receiving the Spirit, and it is only effective if we are not clear what it is that we should expect to happen.

Twice in the New Testament having the Spirit is compared with drunkenness; that will give us a starting-point. Luke believed that being filled with new wine was not the true explanation of the behaviour of the disciples at Pentecost (Acts 2.13), but what showed must have been similar to intoxication, to make the comment plausible; mocking has to be close to the truth if it is to be effective. The other place in the New Testament where the comparison is made is in the Letter to the Ephesians: Do not be drunk with wine . . . but be filled with the Spirit (5.18), and here again the antithesis Wine/Spirit depends on the possibility of comparing and contrasting the result of one with the result of the other.

Our starting-point for looking for the work of the Spirit is the realization that we are unstable creatures, as we know all too well when we drink too much. It is said of people in this state, They are not themselves, today. There must be a long list of kinds of creature that are not so subject to change; but we are.

Nor is alcohol the only cause that effects a change in character; health, friends, enemies, society, public and private events, all may have the result of making us not our usual selves: happier or sadder; more confident or more shy; better or worse.

We are, some more, some less, like the weather, changeable; and the changes in us can be the result of external forces acting upon us. We are not like rocks, or stars, or portraits in a gallery, or anything else of which we say, It is always there, and it is always the same.

This characteristic of human beings is not to be regretted (though it may sometimes make for confusion and annoyance) but to be welcomed and prized highly. It is because we are open to influences that we can be affected by God, filled with the Spirit. We could not believe that this could happen to us, if we did not know how open and mutable our characters are.

To answer the question, Have you received the Spirit?, we need to look for the occasions on which our actions have been better than we had reason to expect. And there is no difficulty in knowing what 'better' means here; Paul gives us a check-list of nine items:

> love, joy, peace,
> patience, kindness, goodness,
> fidelity, gentleness, self-control
> (Galatians 5.22f)

It is frequently the case that we are not ourselves, today; the reason is because we are being led by the Spirit.

SILENCE BEFORE GOD

Trinity Sunday
ASB p.640

ALL the other festivals and seasons of the Christian year relate to events that happened or will happen in time: Advent, Christmas, Epiphany, Lent, Passiontide, Easter, Ascension, Pentecost. Only Trinity Sunday refers to a reality that has no date. There must be an answer to the question, Which year was Jesus crucified?, even if we do not know what the answer is; but it would be nonsense to ask, When did God become the Holy Trinity? That God is always Father, Son and Holy Spirit excludes the idea that at some time or other he began to be so.

One of our practical problems, as we know all too well, is that frequent reference to God makes us over-familiar with the idea of him, in a way that is dangerous and destructive. We have a desire to manage our affairs – domestic, financial, recreational and so on; and this desire is useful and necessary for an ordered life. Can we not also manage the religious aspect of our lives? We assume that we can. That is the mistake.

Trinity Sunday is the essential reminder, coming round once every year, that we cannot manage God. We cannot even imagine him. A god whom we could hold in our minds, in the way that we can hold on to multiplication tables, or elementary geometry, would not be God. All the statements that we make about him are only childish things that will have to be put away; and it is necessary to remember now that they will have to be put away, when we eventually see, face to face.

In the church, in liturgy, theology, and religion; in reading the Bible, teaching R.E., preaching, we are always dealing with more than we can cope with. It must be so, if it is God we are talking about; and it is easy to forget that it must be so, and to start thinking and speaking as though we could manage God, in much the same way that we can manage problems to do with circles and triangles. An important part of the religious attitude has to be, This is beyond me. We are dealing with things too wonderful for us to know, and we speak of things which we do not understand (Job 42.3).

In his account of the vision of God in the temple, Isaiah makes no attempt to describe God: he only says that he was sitting upon a throne, and that his train filled the temple. What we hear about God we overhear from the seraphim. The same method of describing God by allowing the reader to overhear what others say, is used in Revelation, chapter 4, and it is dependent on Isaiah.

We catch the idea of God from other people who, in their turn, caught it from others; and the idea of God is not as simple as a geometric figure; we cannot hold him in our minds or control him by thinking about him. He is unlike all the other ideas we shall ever have, because they are ideas of things in the world, and he is not one of them.

We need Trinity Sunday badly, as a time when we can shake off an over-confident and false familiarity with the Maker and Mender of everything; we need silence before the unimaginable and unmanageable Other.

WE DID NOT ASK TO COME

2nd after Pentecost
ASB p.643

THE parable of the invitations to dinner, specially in its Lucan form (14.16–24), totally undermines the way in which we usually think about the church and our religion. Anyone could be forgiven for supposing that the situation is that some people choose to go to church and find it helpful, whereas others choose to play golf, or watch football, or jog. It is all a matter of what suits you best, and you decide. The parable, however, sees the situation in an entirely different way.

The guests have been given advance notice of the dinner, as was customary (we are told) in both Jewish and Hellenistic society; but when the servants arrived to tell them that everything was ready, they made last-minute excuses: all of them; one and all, it says; not just a proportion of them; not just a small group; the three instances that are given are meant to cover all the guests. The host is therefore faced with everything ready for the meal, and not one single person coming to eat it. He solves his problem by getting in, first the poor and destitute, and then, because there are still empty places, those who live outside the city, the most extreme drop-outs. What motivates him is self-respect: I want my house to be full. It must not be said that he has been put to shame by those who refused to accept his invitation.

The people who do in fact sit down for the dinner really had very little choice; they only came because they were persuaded to come. It was certainly no idea of theirs in the first place; somebody's servant simply turned up unexpectedly and dragged them off. The only choices in the parable are the choices of those who do not come, and do not therefore taste the banquet, as the host himself says at the end.

The parable does nothing, therefore, to encourage us to think that our decisions are all-important, and that God respects the precious gift of freedom with which he has so wonderfully endowed us, and so on. The parable is about people who choose and do not partake, and other people who have no choice and do partake. We are meant to see ourselves in the second group; those who partake without having chosen.

We were made to come in; compelled. One way or another, the message of Jesus, the good news of his death and resurrection, the Bible, the church, the sacraments, people already caught up in it, or something inside us, pulled us in. We could not say, I chose. The only think left to say is, I was chosen.

This is a way of thinking about our faith that is far more full of hope than the alternative, the way in which we usually think about the church and our religion. If we did not ask to come, but found ourselves in, like the people from the hedgerows, then there is every chance that what got us here will also keep us here. Things go wrong with our choices; thank goodness believing was not one of them.

FEAR OR FAITH

3rd after Pentecost
ASB p. 648

J ESUS says to Jairus, Do not be afraid; only show faith. Why did he say, Do not be afraid? – afraid of what?

To find the answer to that question, we shall have to remember first, that the same double miracle, Jairus' daughter and the woman with the haemorrhages, is also in Mark's gospel, and that Luke probably drew it from Mark, making a few small alterations as he did so. In Mark's gospel as a whole, there is a very clear distinction between faith and fear. They are alternatives; you either believe, or you are afraid. The disciples in Mark are frequently said to be afraid, and the book ends with the fear and disobedience of the women at the tomb, who said nothing to anyone because they were afraid (16.8).

Secondly, we need to know that Mark's gospel is a book written for people expecting to be martyred. They will follow Jesus literally (8.34) and drink the cup that he drinks and be baptized with the baptism that he is baptized with (10.38).

There is the greatest concentration of miracle-stories in Mark, of all four gospels; they come with greater frequency there, than in any of the other three. And the reason why this is so may be to do with Mark's being a book for people expecting martyrdom. One of the Old Testament books, probably the last to be written, the Book of Daniel, also has miracle-stories: the fiery furnace in chapter 3 and the lion-pit in chapter 6. These two stories also seem to be there in Daniel to encourage the readers to submit to persecution by the Greek King Antiochus even if it means being put to death. God will raise the dead and bring those who have been faithful to him into his final kingdom and everlasting life (12.2). Both of Daniel's stories refer to the faith of the victims of persecution (3.28, 6.23). Those who put their trust in God will not fear death.

Jairus, therefore, in the gospel story, stands for those who listen as the book is being read; it is to each of them that Jesus says, in the presence of death, Do not be afraid, only show faith. Even if they will not have to suffer martyrdom, there will still be many occasions in their lives that might reduce them to destructive fear and terror, such as the hostility of society towards Christians, sickness, accidents and disasters.

Opposites cannot be present at the same time in the same place; fear and faith are alternatives; if we have faith, we shall not be afraid; when we find ourselves full of fear, then is the time for deeper faith.

THE VARIETY OF THE SCRIPTURES

4th after Pentecost
ASB p.653

IT must be the choice of the Jerusalem Bible translation of Acts 8 that draws our attention to something we might not otherwise have noticed: the particular passage in the scriptures that puzzles the eunuch is one that refers to somebody who had no descendants for anyone to talk about, like the eunuch himself, one assumes. It is an example of the way in which the scriptures work, as Coleridge had noticed and described in his *Confessions of an Inquiring Spirit* (1825): there is a correspondence between the biblical writer and the mind of the reader.

It is unfortunate that in English we often use the singular (Bible, Scripture) whereas in Greek both words are plural (The Books, The Scriptures); the plurality of the books is important, because the way in which they act upon us depends on the differences between their authors; and these differences can be obscured if we refer to the books in general as the word of God, or think of the Holy Spirit as their common inspiration, over-riding the diversity of persons, times and places.

Passages from the scriptures work, by striking us as significant to us, personally and individually, or corporately, in the varied circumstances that we happen to be in at the time. The childless eunuch wants to know whom the prophet is descriinbg as childless; is he talking about himself, or somebody else? Is he perhaps talking about the eunuch who is reading the prophecy? The various prophets have different messages, and different parts even of one book come at us with different force from time to time; Isaiah, for example, whom the eunuch was reading, changes his tone more frequently than any other.

One of the many advantages of a daily lectionary that covers most of the biblical books in a year or two is that through it we store up passages in our memories that may be of no use to us at the time when we read them, but come to life weeks or months later. Just as the shepherd found the sheep and the women the coin, the scriptures find us.

There is an unpredictability about how it will happen. We no more know now what will make sense to us next month than we can forecast how we shall be feeling then. The extraordinary diversity of the material in the books, and the variety of ways of understanding it (there is no such thing as the one and only meaning of a text), provide us with a rich resource. It is like inheriting your father's tool-chest, not knowing what some of the instruments are for, or how to handle them. Maybe there are parts of the scriptures we shall never get round to using; or perhaps that is the wrong way to put it, and we should say that we cannot be sure in advance where the light will break-out next.

If it is true that in all their afflictions he was afflicted and if this was believed by the writers of the books that are gathered together in the canon, then it will not be surprising if from time to time as we read, we find a correspondence between what they wrote and what we need to hear – not surprising, but always a surprise.

LAMBS AMONG WOLVES

5th after Pentecost
ASB p.658

JESUS says to the seventy-two: I am sending you like lambs among wolves (Luke 10.3); it is extraordinary, even worse than the parallel in Matthew who has sheep among wolves (10.16). Lambs will have less chance of escaping; and the pathos is greater, recalling lamb to the slaughter (Isaiah 53.7), and gathering the lambs with his arm and carrying them in his bosom (Isaiah 40.11).

God does not fulfil what we expect of a good employer. He treats his agents abominably. Here they are, being sent off without any protection or provision: Carry no purse or pack, and travel barefoot. The only information they are given in advance is that they are likely to be torn limb from limb and devoured by those to whom they go, as lambs are devoured by wolves.

It is no good blaming the wolves for being wolf-like; that is their nature. It is God who is to blame, because he makes a mock of his agents. He says so, himself:

I frustrate false prophets and their omens, and make fools of diviners;
I reverse what wise men say and make nonsense of their wisdom (Isaiah 44.25).

We expect those who are in authority over us to support us in our decisions: the Head should not let the staff down; the Minister should back up his civil servants; the Chief Constable stand up for the Force. But God does none of these things; he does nothing to cover up for our failures and inadequacies; in fact, it is even worse than that: he changes the rules in the middle of the game, without warning.

The first three verses of Acts 11 describe how Jewish Christians in Jerusalem disputed with Peter because he had visited gentiles and sat at table with them. They complained about Peter's behaviour, because it was, in their view, contrary to God's law. Peter, too, had refused to eat food that was unclean according to the law. There had been no suggestion in the scriptures that the law would be revised or rescinded; Peter and the Jewish Christians in Jerusalem have to be persuaded by events that this must be what has happened; How could I possibly stand in God's way?

It makes it very difficult for us, with a God who acts in this way, ever to appeal to the past and the continuity of tradition. How do we know whether the regulations have been changed? Paul believed that God had abolished the clear command about circumcision in Genesis 17, and had to argue his case in Galatia and at Rome; most Christians now think that God has rescinded the equally clear instruction about women's head-gear in 1 Corinthians 11. The more one reads about the past, the more one sees that what often seemed to people then to be right and good, strikes us as odd and stuffy.

It must be that God has a deliberate policy not to validate the decisions of his agents, but to abandon those whom he sends, like lambs among wolves. This is the opposite of what is said elsewhere: Whatever you forbid on earth shall be forbidden in heaven, and whatever you allow on earth shall be allowed in heaven (Matthew 18.18). Though God's use of us is embarrassing and frustrating, it is much healthier for us to see it this way. It would be fatal if we ever thought that God had handed over his authority to us, and that he would back us whatever we said or did.

SEEING AND FOLLOWING

6th after Pentecost
ASB p.663

MARK tells his stories with the heaviest irony. The healing of Bartimaeus (10.46ff), the gospel for this Sunday, is an example of it. It is the last paragraph before the entry into Jerusalem, and it is the final healing-miracle in the book; the only miracle in Jerusalem will be the cursing of the fig-tree in chapter 11. Mark takes great care how and where he puts the miracles; the first (1.21ff) announced the end of the old order: You have come to destroy us; the last will show us what is to take the place of the synagogue and the law.

Bartimaeus begs for mercy. The word he uses is the same as the *Eleison* we say in the eucharist. Because he does not specify what it is he wants, Jesus asks him what it is he is to do for him. The blind man says, I want my sight back. Jesus says, Go; but the man does not; instead he follows Jesus on the road from Jericho to Jerusalem.

The road, or way (it is the same word in Greek) is a title that Christians used for themselves (e.g. Acts 9.2), and to be a disciple of Jesus is to follow him, to disown oneself, to go to crucifixion, and to lose your life; Mark has explained this clearly to his readers in chapter 8, and we see how the disciples fail to understand it or to do it. Bartimaeus, however, uses his sight to become a follower of Jesus; he goes behind Jesus in the way, and will lose his life in order that he may save it.

Your faith has saved you is therefore extraordinarily ironical in this context. Certainly Bartimaeus is no longer blind; he can see. He can see, to follow; but to follow means to lose your life; and to lose your life means to save it.

As Mark explains Jesus, and what it means to be a follower of

Jesus, the gospel does not provide us with information of the kind that many people in the ancient world were looking for. Paul had said, Greeks look for wisdom, but we proclaim Christ nailed to the cross (1 Corinthians 1.22f.), and this is very similar to Mark's point of view also. The only wisdom or knowledge is the crucifixion of Jesus, and his resurrection. The demons and unclean spirits think that they know who Jesus is, and they address him as The Holy One of God, Son of the Most High God; but Jesus always silences them. Knowing who Jesus is, is not going to save anyone. What matters is knowing what he does, and doing it after him.

The only knowledge that Mark offers is the deserted Jesus, on the cross, asking why God has abandoned him. Those are his last words in this gospel. The gift of sight is for seeing nothing but that, and for seeing it as the one thing that matters. In order to see everything, desire to see nothing but this, and to follow, like Bartimaeus.

LOVE GOD

7th after Pentecost
ASB p.668

T HE first commandment, Jesus says, is to love God; but is not that impossible to imagine, or to do? How could anyone love God? It would make it much easier for us, if we were allowed to say that to love God is to keep his commandments; and that his commandment is that we should love one another. We could understand that, and try to do it; then, by loving God in one another we should have fulfilled the commandment to love God. But would we? Can the first commandment be disposed of by dissolving it into the second? Why would there be a first and a second, if they were really both the same?

There is a point of great importance here, and if we miss it, much trouble will follow. For example, religion provides us with strong attachments; we become devoted to particular places, where we think prayer has been valid; even to particular areas within a church (my pew, where I have always sat); we can only be happy with certain versions of the Prayer Book, or of the scriptures; particular ways of doing the services, and an unending list of what we like. To say that it is God we must love, with all our heart and soul and mind and strength, is to say No to all religious attachments. Just as it is sometimes said that somebody is in love with love, so it is possible to be in love with religion, not with God. God is none of the things we like, because he is not a thing at all.

How can we love one who is not like us? – that is the problem, or so we think. But it is not as much of a problem as you might suppose. Anyone who loves anyone knows that the person loved is other than themselves, with different ideas, different reactions, different tastes, even a different sense of humour. The relationship will go very wrong, if this is ignored; it seems almost to be the case that difference is essential to loving, a necessity; certainly some of the happiest friendships and marriages are those between people who seem to outsiders to be complete opposites.

In loving God, difference is at its maximum. His ideas, reactions, tastes, sense of humour and so on are completely different from ours. But this does not prevent us from loving him; it only makes the relationship more demanding, and more rewarding.

What do we love, when we love God? He is beyond all the things in the world, and different from them, and far better than they are. We cannot say of anything that we can hold in our minds, This is God. The world and things in the world may be stepping-stones towards God; loving it and them may be a beginning that will lead us towards loving God himself. But at some point the stepping-stones will stop, and we shall have to go further, beyond anything imaginable, into a direct relationship with the author and maker of everything; and this going further will require all our heart, and all our soul and all our mind and all our strength. The totality that is required of us corresponds to the total difference between God and us; nothing else makes such a demand.

LOVE YOUR ENEMIES

8th after Pentecost
ASB p.673

IF Jesus had only told us to love, we should not have thought it impossible. It would not have been difficult for us to convince ourselves that we were really loving people, full of good-will towards everybody. The way we should have done it would have been to adapt our attitudes to people we meet and know, according to how they relate to us: warmth and affection towards some, with a gradual cooling-off towards others, and then a cut-out point, beyond which there would be people of whom we would say, I do not know them at all; they are not my sort of person. If all we were commanded was to love, we might think we could do it.

But what Jesus says is, Love your enemies; do good to those who hate you; bless those who curse you; pray for those who treat you spitefully (Luke 6.27f). Even so, we must be careful that we do not evade the issue, because our immediate defensive reaction is to say, I have no enemies; there is no one, so far as I know, who hates me; I am unaware that anyone is cursing me or treating me spitefully. I am not the sort of person who attracts hostility; so there is no problem, for me.

There is a group of people, however, to whom we find it very difficult to relate in a positive way. We may not call them enemies, or think of them as hating us, cursing us or treating us spitefully. But they are people with whom we cannot get on. The trouble is, they do not like us; they show no sign of pleasure when they meet us; they signal, in one way or another, that they would rather be with somebody else: looking over our left shoulders at the people behind us at parties; changing their facial expressions when someone else joins the group, so that we see that they are no longer bored; they become animated, interested, life has begun again for them, when a different person is in their sights. They regard us as belonging to an uninteresting species, because we are housewives who do not go out to work, or secretaries, or accountants, or clergymen.

The warmth of our affection for people diminishes according to their response to us; or, it may be more accurate to say, according to what we think is their response to us. We imagine ourselves standing at the centre of concentric circles of decreasing intensity, like the ripples on a flat surface of water. And we think that this is how it must be; it is inevitable. How could we love those who do not love us?

Jesus does not command love in general, but love for our enemies in particular; and this alters the picture we must have. We are not at a centre, with other people further and further from us, placed there by us, according to our idea of their attitude to us. We are to take the people for whom we have no time and who, we think, have no time for us but find us boring, wrong-headed, superstitious, out of touch – the people we try to avoid: these are the people we are commanded to love, to do good to, to put ourselves at the disposal of; we are even to lend them our property, without expecting them to return it.

It is not a pleasant prospect. But we can remember how, when we were young and awkward, there were people who overcame their displeasure and treated us far better than we deserved. How they helped us, and gave us confidence. It can be done; and we know it can be done, because someone did it to us. There is such a thing as *Agape*. God can motivate us into exercising it. It is a powerful force that breaks down all kinds of opposition. We are committed to believing that it is almighty and that in the end, with us or without us, it will bring everything to fulfilment. There are no cut-off points, and no one is beyond its reach.

Can these bones live? we wonder. They can. It happened to us; it can happen through us.

DEATH IS OVERCOME BY DEATH

9th after Pentecost
ASB p.678

A PERSISTENT though now rather unfashionable tradition invites us to see the Christian life as warfare. We are manfully to fight under Christ's banner, against sin, the world, and the devil, and to continue Christ's faithful soldiers and servants unto our life's end. For this warfare we shall need the whole armour of God, and that is this Sunday's theme. But the trouble is that the description of the armour does not make it sound as though it would be very effective; Paul, in one of the earliest instances of this theme, says that it is faith and love for breast-plate, and hope for helmet (1 Thessalonians 5.8); we think we shall need more than that, if we are to overcome the power of evil.

God's warfare, however, is not to be pursued with weapons of power, but with powerlessness. The story of David and Goliath hints at this: David cannot slay the giant with Saul's equipment; he trusts in God, and uses what he has to hand, a sling and a stone.

The solution to our problems that is the heart of Christianity has elegance; it is ingeniously simple and effective. The method by which everything is put right is through using what has, apparently, gone wrong. Every living thing exists by destroying something else; and to submit to destruction is the way in which destruction is overcome. Paul writes to the Corinthians about endurance; that is the only recommendation that he can offer, because there is nothing more important than acceptance of what is, apparently, against one's interests and prosperity. The weapons of righteousness do not defend us from evil or enable us to destroy it: they lay us open to its force, and they destroy us (2 Corinthians 6.3–10).

The healing of the boy with the deaf and dumb spirit illustrates how submission to the attack is also the victory over it; accepting the disease is also its cure. The spirit had been trying to destroy the boy by throwing him into the fire and into water; and Jesus' words appear to have had the same effect on him: the boy looked like a corpse; in fact, many said, He is dead (Mark 9.14–29).

We are saved by the destruction of Jesus, and by sharing in it. We are baptized into his death; faith, love and hope are the ways in which we put to death all that is in us that is not of God. God uses destruction to save us from destruction; by death, death is overcome.

The armour of God is an odd sort of armour, because it protects you from nothing; it only exposes you all the more to what you are fighting against.

GOD IS NOT MOCKED

10th after Pentecost
ASB p.683

THE great danger with religion is that you can end up thinking that you can use it to fool God. Paul has to shake the Galatians out of this false idea; there is no system of religious practice that we can adopt, whereby God can be deceived by us, and we can control him and compel him to do our will.

Simon, who had invited Jesus to a meal (Luke 7.36ff.) is given as an example of a religious person who has got it all wrong. He thinks that the woman who is weeping and kissing Jesus' feet is a sinner, and that Jesus himself is no prophet because he does not know who or what she is; but he is wrong on both counts: the woman is acting in this way because she is forgiven much; and it is Simon himself who has been forgiven little. The trouble with Simon is that he lacks self-knowledge. He has ignored the normal duties of a host: washing the feet of his guest; greeting him with a kiss; anointing his head. But he is totally unaware of this; all he has time for is to criticize Jesus and the woman.

False religion is self-deluding, leading us to suppose that we can fool God into thinking less than the truth about us, and that we are more important than we are (Galatians 6.1ff.). Hence Paul's injunction, Look to yourself.

Self-knowledge is easier to preach about, or to write about, than to practise. It is recognized as the mark of genuineness by all the major religions; what we must long for is the removal of the veil that conceals from us what our present state really is. We are happy to be deceived about ourselves; what we fear is self-awareness.

The three passages set for this Sunday all stress the close connection between being and doing: David has treated Saul well; Saul has treated David badly. We reap what we sow; that is, we shall be judged on what we have done. You only need to see what the woman did, and what Simon did not do, to see who has been forgiven much, and who has been forgiven little. We are what we do.

Whatever is meant by justification by faith and not by works of the law, it is not that the close link between being and doing has been abolished. We cannot excuse the absence of good deeds from our lives, by appealing to a doctrine of faith instead of works (as the author of the Letter of James saw so well). A false step in theology at this point leads to endless self-delusion. Plain common-sense is a far better guide than pseudo-piety. Deeds still speak louder than words.

WAIT AND SEE

11th after Pentecost
ASB p.688

CHRISTIANITY operates with the minimum information about the future. If someone were to ask us, What do you know about what will happen to you when you have died?, we should have to say that we know nothing for certain. Hopes and expectations that were expressed in some parts of the New Testament did not happen in the way that the writers thought they would. Paul thought that not all of his contemporaries would die before the end of the world, but they did.

This ignorance of the future must seem to be a deficiency in a religion; what can I look forward to? must be the question we all ask, and we feel we have a right to an answer. Matthew's parable of the labourers in the vineyard (20.1ff.) is preceded by Peter's questions, What about us?, How shall we fare?

The parable shows that we cannot hold God to a course of action that we think appropriate for him to follow. The people employed at the beginning of the day assumed that pay would be on an hourly basis; but they were wrong to make this assumption. The employer is free to do what he likes with his own money; he can be kinder than he needs to be, if he wants. He can overthrow our expectations.

It is simply a fact that we have no information about life after death, the end of the world, the life of the age to come. And it is right that we should not have this information. It is not a defect in Christianity that it leaves us in ignorance about the future; nor should we try to make good what we have not been given, by speculation or by any other means. Our relationship with God does not allow us to have certainty about what is to happen to the world and to us, because it is a relationship of trust and hope, and this excludes foreseeing and knowing in advance; we have to be ignorant, in order to rely on God totally.

All we have is our present relationship with God and our experience of him in the past; there is faith in God, and this sets some limits to what can legitimately be expected. If we think he has dealt with us generously, in calling us into existence and in his dealings with us so far, we can hardly think that he will be different in the future. The saying about the last and the first discourages us from forming specific expectations; but it does not permit us to think that God will be unfair. The one whom we have learnt to trust will still deal with us on that basis, and that must be the only answer we can give to the question, What are you looking forward to? How shall we fare? We must simply wait and see.

SALT AND LIGHT

12th after Pentecost
ASB p.693

THE sayings about salt and the light of the world in this week's gospel (Matthew 5.13–16) are so familiar that they make no impact on us when we read them. In such circumstances, one solution is to go back to the original context from which the four verses have been abstracted to provide us with the Sunday reading, and see from that what the evangelist thought they meant; he was an author who paid close attention to arrangement, and it is often through observing this that we gain insight into meaning.

John the Baptist and Jesus have both said that the Kingdom of Heaven has drawn near; that is, the time when God will rule, and abolish all that is contrary to his will; to survive, one must change one's ways, repent. But change them in which direction? The beatitudes answer the question: those who will enter the kingdom are those who are poor in spirit, sorrowful, gentle, hungry and thirsty for right to prevail, merciful, pure in heart, peacemakers, persecuted. They will share in God's rule, be consoled by him, possess the earth, and so on.

The rest of the discourse (ending in 7.27) can be read as a commentary on the beatitudes, taken in the reverse order; certainly the final beatitude is about persecution and the next paragraph picks up that theme (7.11f.): the disciples will be persecuted, just as the prophets had been persecuted in Old Testament times. They will be persecuted, because they will be different from other people; and they will be different, because they will believe different things and live in a different way. They will be as different from their contemporaries as salt is different from whatever it is used to salt, or as light is different from darkness. To be persecuted, there must be distinctions: no one persecutes those who share their views. The disciples must be different from other people.

To give substance to this difference it will help if we go back to the beatitudes and read them again, asking the question, How do those sayings compel us to be different from what we should have been if we had never heard them? We should never have thought that poverty was blessed, or mourning, or any of the other descriptions of discipleship. Living out of God and waiting for him to rule the world call for a style of life that is unlike what we take to be getting on in the world and doing well.

The disciples are like salt and light, because they have the wisdom that Jesus has given them, to know that the way things are in the world now is not the way that they should be, or eventually will be. The disciples are people in revolt; they have withdrawn from the race; they do not share the hopes of the rest. But, they believe, the future lies with them; and the rest will, in the end, see that this is so. It is part of the responsibility of the disciples that others should come to agree with them eventually.

YOU WILL KNOW WHAT TO SAY

13th after Pentecost
ASB p.698

THE difficulty about the New Testament is that it says more than we think it should. The promises that are made in it seem to us excessive and the assurances that are given seem unwise. If we had been writing it today, we should have been more circumspect; hindsight would have saved us from making the mistakes that too much zeal and confidence have led to; or so we think.

There is a glaring example in today's gospel. Jesus tells the Twelve (and therefore, presumably, all those whom he sends to preach the coming Kingdom) not to worry how to speak or what to say; the content (what to say) will be given to them when the time comes, and they need not be concerned about the method (how to speak) because it will be the Spirit of their Father who will be speaking in them (Matthew 10.19,20).

Our anxiety about this passage is due partly to the idea that it might encourage people to think that there is no need to prepare sermons or addresses or talks or intercessions; and even more to the conclusion that might be drawn, that what we say is always God's word and has his authority and so is always right and true. There would be no room for discussion with those who took this view of their pronouncements; to any question we might raise, they would reply: It is not I who say this, but the Spirit of my Father speaking in me, as Jesus said he would.

This is a further reason for being ill at ease with this passage in Matthew's gospel; it seems that the evangelist has adapted a paragraph in Mark (13.9–13), and there the promise is less specific: When the time comes, Jesus says, say whatever is given you to say, for it is not you who will be speaking, but the Holy Spirit. Mark does not have Matthew's words, *in you*; and in Mark, the Spirit does speak on the day of Jesus' trial before Pilate, but he speaks through Pilate, the soldiers, the passers-by, and so on; not through Jesus, and certainly not through his disciples.

We have therefore plenty of reasons to feel embarrassed at the promise Jesus makes to the disciples in Matthew's gospel; it seems to us to say too much; it goes too far; it sanctions excessive confidence in our own ideas and their expression.

But this is all a mistake. We are, as usual, asking the wrong question and forcing a passage in the gospels into saying what the author never meant. The starting-point for reading this discussion in Matthew 10 should be far away from where we began; the hearers of the discourse are those who are put on the spot because they are asked to say what they believe, by hostile critics who can mock them and injure them. To arrive at the right place to hear this promise correctly, I shall have to say to myself, Have I the courage to say what I believe, and have I the sense to know how to put it? Will I be able to stand the trouble it will cause if I do speak what I believe is the truth, and dare I trust myself to do it without making a fool of myself and of the cause in which I hope I believe? The encouragement of Matthew's promise here in his gospel is addressed to people who are desperate, and at their wits' end; they know what they should do, but they doubt their ability to do it. They are the only people who will understand what is being said.

WAITING FOR GOD

14th after Pentecost
ASB p.703

IN what sense is it true that: The one who asks always receives (Luke 11.10)? The purpose of this saying in this Sunday's gospel, which includes also the Lucan version of the Lord's Prayer and the parable of the friend at midnight (who got what he wanted because of his persistence, not his friendship), is to encourage us to practice petitionary prayer. Why should we ask, search and knock?

Suppose we said, The reason why we shall always have to be petitioners is because we never get any better; we are always in the position of beggars. We make no moral progress, but continue to be as we were when we were children; old age only brings out our infant faults in a clearer light. True, but it is not what is said. What is said is that the one who asks always receives; whereas asking has made no difference to us; we are the same, we have not received what we asked for.

Or suppose we said, Our concern is the world, and it never gets any better, only worse: more violence, more hunger, more misery. We have to ask God for peace and equity and justice, and to go on asking. But still this is not the reason that the text gives; we are saying we have to go on asking because God does not give what we ask for, not because he does.

Or suppose we said, Asking is its own justification; it brings us into our proper relationship with God, creature with Creator. We are beggars, and must always ask for mercy. This is so, but it is still not what the text says. We are not told to ask because it is good for us to come to God in this way, but because those who ask always receive. And the plain fact is that they do not.

A better solution is to go back to the Lord's Prayer, to which Luke has appended these sayings and the parable of the persistent friend. The prayer asks for God's name to be held holy and for his kingdom to come: that is, for the end of the world as it is now, and for the end of us as we are now; it is a petition for the final act of God, beseeching him to make everything new, us included. The Lord's Prayer belongs to the world of apocalyptic, and apocalyptic is the way people think who are at the end of their tether. They know that what is needed is not a re-jigging of the way things are now: a change of government, a new policy, a revised plan; but total revolution, with God in control; he must take over from all governments and rule his world directly. Apocalyptic is the way of thinking that comes from a final and universal scepticism about the possibility of human beings ever being just in their dealings with one another. Your kingdom come means, You must rule, not us; not any of us.

This is the asking that is valid and that is being encouraged here. And it is being encouraged by the promise that it will be answered, because it will happen; God's rule will come. The followers of Jesus are the genuinely ridiculous people who have gone on for centuries saying this prayer and waiting for an event that has not happened yet. If we minimize the folly of it, we lose the point of it, and settle for something less, easier to explain and, eventually, boring because inadequate. If we do not want God or think we shall have him, we are not being ourselves.

GOD AS KING

15th after Pentecost
ASB p.708

AT bottom, we are all anarchists, calling no man Lord, despising politics and politicians, and imagining that the ideal state would be one in which no one would have authority over us, but everyone would be their own ruler. It is odd that it should be so, in a religion that undoubtedly began with the idea of God as king, and soon developed to include Jesus as his agent and representative, and looked forward with longing to the time in the future when he would come to govern the universe, and every knee would bow to him. The post-communion sentence expresses it thus: The kingdom of the world is to become the kingdom of our Lord and of his Christ, and he shall reign for ever (Revelation 11.15).

How can we, whose attitude to authority is so negative, pray for those in authority, as we are asked to do this Sunday? How can we value good government when we secretly believe that all government is temporary and evil, and long for the time when it will be abolished for good and all?

The majority of the New Testament writers looked at it in a different way. They were not anarchists, but believed that government was good and necessary. God would rule, and the sooner the better; he had appointed a human being, descended from King David, whom he had exalted to his right hand, to be Lord of the universe, and he had given him all authority. Meanwhile, until the end of this age, he had given temporary

173

authority to rulers: emperors, governors, magistrates and so on. Christians, they believed, were to obey them, as the agents of God; and to pray for them, that everyone might lead a tranquil and quiet life in full observance of religion and high standards of morality (1 Timothy 2.1ff).

The one New Testament writing that adopts a different point of view is Revelation. John is unique among the New Testament writers in believing that the Roman Empire is diabolical and its emperors evil beasts who are not to be obeyed. John is for civil disobedience, and the martyrdom that must follow. But he is aware that he is out of step with others – the followers of one Nicolas, whom he calls Balaamites and Jezebelites, people who believed in compromise with the Roman authorities and the positive good of the secular power (Revelation 2, 3). Nevertheless, even John does not doubt that authority itself is good and necessary; how else could he call Jesus King of kings and Lord of lords? And at the end of the book, he sees the kings of the earth bringing their splendour to the Holy City.

Herod, Matthew said, had put the Baptist in prison because he had told him that he had no right to Herodias, his brother Philip's wife (14.3,4). Herod would not be told, as they used to say to us when we were children (and later, too): You wont be told, will you? The question that today's readings raise is whether we think the final and ideal condition is not to need to be told; do we think that we shall cease to be beings that will always need to be ruled and governed by one who is other than ourselves?

Our present need of good government is a reminder of our permanent need of God as ruler. We pray for those in authority because we need them, and because they show us what we really are.

WHO IS MY NEIGHBOUR?

16th after Pentecost
ASB p.713

WHEN Jesus was asked what was the first of all the commandments, Mark says he quoted two: You must love the Lord your God (Deuteronomy 6.4ff) and, You must love your neighbour as yourself (Leviticus 19.18; Mark 12.28f). And when he was asked for a definition of *neighbour*, Luke says that he replied with the parable of the Good Samaritan (10.25–37); the neighbour is anyone who happens to be around – there is no closer definition of him than that. But in the fourth gospel, the word *neighbour* is replaced by *one another* (e.g. I give you a new commandment: love one another. John 13.34) and in the Johannine Letters, by *brother* (e.g. Anyone who says, I love God, and hates his brother is a liar, since a man who does not love the brother that he has seen, cannot love God, whom he has never seen (I John 4.20)).

The words *brother* and *sister* are technical terms, meaning members of the church. The New English Bible uses the expression *fellow-Christian* to translate them. It is because of this substitution of *one another* or *brother* for neighbour that it is often said that whereas Jesus taught that God's command was that we should love whoever happened to be at hand, with no questions asked, the church gradually restricted our obligations to love for fellow members of the institution.

But there is another way of looking at it, and it requires only a modicum of cynicism (which in any case might be described as realism). Which is harder, to love your pagan neighbour, or to love your fellow-Christian? Surely it is the fellow-Christian that it is harder to love, unless he happens to think like you. The real problems come with those whose understanding of the faith is different from ours; who use the same scriptures, the same sacraments, the same words, but mean something different by

175

them. We get more angry with those with whom we feel we ought to agree, than with those who do not raise such expectations in us. The people we want to burn are those whom we think of as heretics, not those who are unbelievers.

The reason we find our fellow-Christians hard to love is because they threaten us and the way we understand our religion and practise it. They do this, at the core and centre of what we believe. They read the same Bible, but hear a different message; they worship the same God (they say) but he means something different to them. They believe in another Jesus, and they are led by another Spirit. It is those who are closest to us who offend us most; those who should be our friends who wound us most severely.

The writer of the Johannine Letters was well aware that this was so, because he lived in a community that had divided, some of its members breaking away from others on doctrinal issues. But he does not think that the command to love your neighbour, or even to love one another, extends to loving those who have gone out from us. They never were really of us, he says; they were always of the world and the evil one.

The question that this raises is, Does Jesus' instruction to love your neighbour include the difficult obligation of loving the fellow-Christian with whom you disagree? Does the history of Christian disagreements (in Eastern Europe, Northern Ireland, the Middle East, for example) encourage us to continue to deal with differences of doctrine through making divisions amoung the brethren? What kind of division is compatible with the command to love?

SPACE FOR DOING

17th after Pentecost
ASB p.717

O F course it is all a matter of getting the balance right, but even so there is no need, ever, to denigrate people as mere activists or write them off as do-gooders. One important element in Christ's religion is action: Not everyone who says ... but only those who do ... (Matthew 7.21). The goodness that we ask to be nurtured in us (in today's collect) must involve us in activity as well as attitudes; and the proof of faith (which is this Sunday's theme) is works. Luke saw that the right question to ask is, What are we to do? (Acts 2.37; compare 16.30, 22.10), and he believed that the answer had already been given: Go and do as he did (Luke 10.37).

God provides us with space for doing, just as he also withdraws from our sight in order that we may have room for believing; and in both cases, it is for the same reason: He will not compel or dominate, because he wants us to be ourselves, and for that we shall need a degree of independence of him and distance from him. We should not think of his withdrawal from us and our distance from him as regrettable, but as necessary and entirely for our good; they are expressions of his total love and approval of us. It is because he wants us to be free creatures, that he protects our independent existence as he does; he loves our liberty and defends it, as we can see from the manner of our salvation. Christ's teaching and his death move us without forcing us; they appeal to our wills and call forth our gratitude.

The extent to which our activity is required is extraordinary. Everything waits to be discovered; nothing pushes itself forward or announces its existence of itself. One wonders why God did not break his own rules and inform us centuries ago of, for example, the causes of infant mortality and the means of reducing it; in this way he could have prolonged millions of lives and saved bottles of tears. But no; our independence and freedom, initiative and activity, are rated more highly than anything else.

Again, one wonders why there is no intervention to prevent the misuse of freedom when it causes suffering to others – cruelty, slavery and genocide. We would welcome tighter controls; we would happily surrender a tyrant's ability to wipe out a large section of humanity, or the possibility of reducing the number of species on the planet, for a world in which there was less freedom.

The fact is that we do not live in a controlled world which either announces its own regulations in advance, or steps in to restrict our actions and their results. Our independence is highly valued by God, who protects it and ensures it. There would be no reality in his final Well done, had we not really done well.

A LIVING SACRIFICE

18th after Pentecost
ASB p.722

GOOD liturgy always says more than you mean; that is what makes it good. A liturgy that expressed no more than our mundane and limited hopes and fears would be so bad as to be unusable. The trouble with liturgy is not that it says too much, but that we may not notice that it is doing so. Take, for example, the ASB post-communion prayer: We offer you our souls and bodies to be a living sacrifice. What would it be like, to be a living sacrifice? And if we knew, would we want to do it?

The expression goes back, through the 1662 first post-communion prayer (And here we offer and present unto thee, O Lord, ourselves, our souls and bodies, to be a reasonable, holy, and lively sacrifice unto thee), to the Letter of Paul to the Romans:

That ye present your bodies a living sacrifice, holy, acceptable unto God, which is your reasonable service (12.1).

What Paul was mainly trying to persuade the Christians in Rome to do, when he wrote this letter in the early 60s of the first century, was, it seems, to agree to a way of getting those who had been Jews to accept those who had never been Jews and had no intention of observing the whole of the law of Moses, including circumcision, the dietary laws and the sacred calendar of feasts and sabbaths; and likewise those who had been gentiles to accept membership of a society in which there would also be Jewish members who continued to keep the law. He sets out his plan in chapters 14 and 15; the earlier part of the letter is the necessary theological foundation for it. Both the Jewish believers and the gentile believers will have to make concessions, and give up what they might be tempted to think were principles. Both sides would see themselves as living sacrifices.

Each group would be abandoning the support and comfort that they derived from living in close proximity with people who shared the same views. We huddle together for encouragement, and look for it where it will come most readily – from people who think like us. All this would go, if we were to join a society that cut across the distinction between Jew and non-Jew, radical and conservative, fundamentalist and liberal. To be a living sacrifice would be like being a permament exile from home, living among people of another tradition whose ideas and customs one did not share, and accepting them as equals.

This is what we ask to be: we ask to be those who have cut themselves off from their origins and background, even from their most prized religious convictions, to be free for one another in a new way, that makes groups, parties and movements completely out of place. This is being a living sacrifice, and it is not at all a pleasant prospect; it is not what we want.

GOD ACTS FIRST

19th after Pentecost
ASB p.728

WE are justified by faith, Paul says (Romans 5.1), coining a phrase that became famous; and we can see how he came to develop this formulation. He borrowed the words from the scriptures (Genesis 15.6 and Habakkuk 2.4), but the idea was an explanation of certain facts. In the churches he had founded, there were Jews and gentiles; some continued to keep the law of Moses, others did not; but the gifts of the Spirit and the fruit of the Spirit were shared among them all; Paul writes: Anyone who does not possess the Spirit of Christ does not belong to Christ (Romans 8.9). One thing they all had in common: they all believed that Jesus was Lord and that God had raised him from the dead, and they had been baptized in that faith.

While we were sinners, Christ died; while we were enemies, we were reconciled to God. What God did, and what Jesus did, came first; faith was the acceptance of what had already happened. And faith was all that was needed. Of course it would show itself in action, otherwise it would not really be faith; but it evidently did not require the believers to keep the law of Moses: gentiles had received the Spirit, simply because they believed; no other explanation was possible, and no other explanation was needed.

The gospel is good news because it is about what has been done for us, for everybody, apart from us, before we knew about it. Before God made us, he loved us, and in that love we were made.

TRUE NARROWNESS

20th after Pentcost
ASB p.733

I F to apply principle without allowance for circumstance is to
be doctrinaire, then Paul was the last person who should be
described in this way. He tells us himself that he adapted his way
of life to the circumstances imposed on him by his mission,
living like a Jew when he was with Jews, and like a gentile when
he was with gentiles. In this respect he could properly be said to
have been a man who had no principles; it was all a matter of
indifference whether you kept the law or not; what mattered
was something else.

It is extraordinary that Paul could write about himself like this,
when we remember that probably only a few years earlier he
had told the gentile Christians in Galatia that if they started to
keep the law, they would sever their connection with Christ
(Galatians 5.2–6). Then, he had said that they were free from the
law; now, he is saying that he is free to keep it, or not to keep it,
according to the circumstances he is in. He not only adapts his
practice, he also adapts his doctrine. You might say he was a
situational theologian.

He is free, he says to make himself anybody's slave. This is the root of
what he says and what he does. His model is Christ, who did just the
same: he was rich, yet he became poor, so that through his poverty
we might become rich (2 Corinthians 8.9). Adaptation to the needs
of others is the law of Christ, and it is the only law that applies.

This is the narrow gate and the narrow road that Jesus teaches
(Matthew 7.13–27). True narrowness is not the strict application
of a detailed set of doctrines; true narrowness is having one idea,
and only one: what Paul calls: The gospel (All this I do for the
gospel's sake); that Christ died for everybody, he gave up
everything for everybody. The implication of this is that we can

no longer put our preferences or our traditions before what is loving. If Christ was made sin for us (2 Corinthians 5.21) what may we not have to do for him?

PURE HOPE

21st after Pentecost
ASB p.738

Do we know anything about life after death? Some people think they do, and quote the experience of those who have recovered from illness, and the messages they say they have received from friends and relations who have died. Others, perhaps the majority, are not persuaded.

There is much to be said for the opinion that we have no information at all about life after death. There is something very attractive about the idea that God has no favourites and that he has not broken his self-imposed silence on this subject, even for the benefit of any of the saints. We all live under the same rule, that we know nothing for sure about our future. Moreover it may be right to deduce from this that we ought not to try to find out; the silence of God is for our good, and a result of his love. He has prepared this situation for us, that we shall all come to the moment of death without knowledge of the future, in order that we may make the offering of our lives, and of our thanks for them, without any further information and without the complication of thinking about rewards and punishments. Hope is purified by absence of knowledge.

As far as knowing what will happen goes, our position is no different from that of Job:

Naked I came from the womb,
naked I shall return whence I came.
The Lord gives and the Lord takes away;
blessed be the name of the Lord (Job 1.21).

Christian hope is trusting in God, without specifying what will happen. To see something (or to know what will happen) is no longer to hope: why hope for what is already seen? (Romans 8.24). God has kept us all in the dark, in order that we may wait with the purest hope.

22nd after Pentecost
(See Year One – Page 89)

BEAR YOUR OWN BURDEN

Last Sunday after Pentecost
ASB p.745

WE listen to the parable of the ten bridesmaids (today's gospel, Matthew 25.1–13) and we think, Those prudent ones are no models for us; they should have shared what oil they had with those who had none; or else they should have offered to go to the shops themselves to buy more. We do not admire their self-concern; this attitude, we think, is totally out of place when it comes to salvation and damnation.

Quite right, too. But the mistake is to identify ourselves with the prudent girls; the parable only works if you identify yourself with the foolish.

Of course you can hope that the prayers of the saints will support you, and of course the saints will pray for the rest of us, that we may be forgiven. The mistake comes when we misuse this hope, and say to ourselves, There is no need for me to repent; others will do it for me.

The parable destroys sham religion: the apparent profession of faith, in order not to do anything about the situation. Give us some of your oil.

There is an extraordinary passage at the end of Paul's letter to the Galatians, in which he says, within the space of four verses, both: Carry one another's burdens, and: Everyone has his own burden to bear (Galatians 6.2–5). Both are true and must be accepted: that we are to be willing to do everything for one another, and that we are to do what we can for ourselves. Compassion does not destroy responsibility, nor does responsibility exclude compassion.

We do not know how much other people can do for us. The saints, the church and Christ all pray for us, we believe. But it would be a mistake (a dangerous and evil mistake) to take this to mean that we have leave off all attention to what we should do. We have not understood what it is to be loved, if we think it excuses us from loving.